THE SAME FATE
as the POOR

THE SAME FATE
as the POOR

Judith M. Noone, M.M.

ORBIS BOOKS

Maryknoll, New York 10545

The Catholic Foreign Mission Society of America (Maryknoll) recruits and trains people for overseas missionary service. Through Orbis Books, Maryknoll aims to foster the international dialogue that is essential to mission. The books published, however, reflect the opinions of their authors and are not meant to represent the official position of the society.

Cataloging-in-Publication Data is available from the Library of Congress, Washington, D. C.

In living memory
of the seventy-five thousand men, women, and children
who died during a decade of violence in El Salvador.

"Christ invites us not to fear persecution because, believe me, brothers and sisters, those who are committed to the poor must risk the same fate as the poor, and in El Salvador we know what the fate of the poor signifies: to disappear, to be tortured, to be captive, and to be found dead."

—Archbishop Oscar Arnulfo Romero
1917-1980

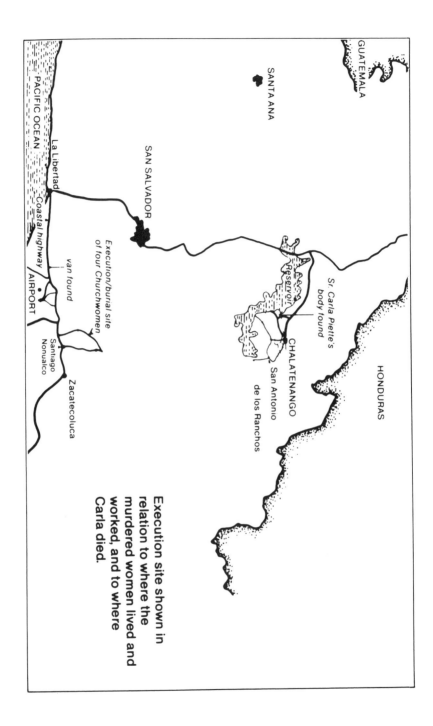

Execution site shown in relation to where the murdered women lived and worked, and to where Carla died.

GUATEMALA

HONDURAS

SANTA ANA

PACIFIC OCEAN

La Libertad

Coastal highway

SAN SALVADOR

AIRPORT

van found

Execution/burial site
of four Churchwomen

Santiago
Nonualco

Zacatecoluca

Reservoir

Sr. Carla Piette's
body found

CHALATENANGO

San Antonio
de los Ranchos

Contents

Preface to the Revised Edition

Judith M. Noone, MM

It has been fifteen years since we received the chilling news of the disappearance of four of our sisters and friends in El Salvador on December 2, 1980: Maura Clarke, MM, Ita Ford, MM, Dorothy Kazel, OSU, and Jean Donovan, lay missioner from the Diocese of Cleveland. Even before the news was confirmed we began to receive urgent requests for press statements, biographical data, and photographs from news agencies and others seeking clues about the lives that ended in such a brutal fashion in an unmarked common grave.

As the weeks, months, and years went by the requests have continued. Interest in the lives and deaths of these women, as well as Ita Ford's friend and co-worker, Maryknoll Sister Carol Piette, who drowned in El Salvador in September 1980, has increased rather than diminished with time. Every year, thousands of communities throughout the world celebrate the anniversary of their deaths in ritual and prayer. Children, streets, parks, and community centers have been named after them in Central America as well as in the United States. In the Bushwick area of their native Brooklyn, for instance, Sisters Mary Burns, SC, and Mary Babic, NDS, founded the Maura Clarke/Ita Ford Center in 1994 to provide education for economically disadvantaged women.

This book was written and first published in 1985 to satisfy the growing demand for a deeper understanding of the three Maryknoll women who laid down their lives for their friends in the embattled nation of El Salvador. Several printings of the book were quickly depleted. Requests for copies have been constant over the years and have come from a wide spectrum of people: students with an interest in the political consequences of living a committed Christian life in today's world; feminist writers wanting to compile biographies of contemporary women; friends and relatives of the women; people of all walks of life, young and old, who were moved by their story and wished to know more about the faith that motivated their lives and led to their deaths.

Fifteen years have served, as all history does, to clarify the past and to expand its context. With the new information provided by the United Nations Truth Commission set up by the Peace Accords of January 1991, it seemed appropriate to issue a new revised edition of *The Same Fate as the Poor*. We are grateful to Orbis Books for accepting the task, and to the Ford and Keogh families for their support and encouragement.

While the original text of the book remains unchanged, save for a few minor corrections, appendices have been added: sections of the Truth Commission Report and the U.S. State Department's Panel on El Salvador related to the murder of the churchwomen, and an update and political analysis of events in Salvador from 1980 to the present by Margaret Swedish of the Religious Task Force on Central America.

Without exception, these official inquiries have verified what we and the families of the women maintained all along—that the murders were ordered by senior officials in the Salvadoran army and covered up by leading members of the military and government of El Salvador—a government which had the military and financial backing of the U.S. government through the blood decade of the 1980s.

May this volume keep alive the timeless message of our friends and sisters who shared the same fate as 75,000 Salvadorans who were murdered in that decade. And may the truth heal and set us free from a history of death and deceit.

San Pedro Sacatepequez, Guatemala
Holy Week 1995

Foreword to the Original Edition

MELINDA ROPER, MM
Community President, 1978-84

When you finish reading this book you will have met three women of faith; three women whose faith was a gift that permeated their personalities, their relationships, and their mission. The manner and moments of their deaths were extraordinary for most of us from the U.S. because we were not attuned to the reality of martyrdom in our world today.

As you read from the letters of Carla, Ita, and Maura; as you understand their love for the peoples of Chile, Nicaragua, and El Salvador; as you comprehend the vision and hope of these three women of faith, your life and faith will be renewed. The inescapable challenge of their lives and deaths is their compassion for and solidarity with the poor. They were not blind to the evil and sin in our world, nor were they naive about its causes. The wisdom of their faith was that their lives were not focused against evil and sin but upon the holiness of human life. Their wisdom flowed from the person, message, life, death, and resurrection of Jesus.

The starkness of their lives and deaths calls us to open our lives to the ultimate simplicity of the gospel:

"There is no greater love than this: to lay down one's life for one's friends." (John 15:13)

"Blessed are you poor . . .
Blessed are you who hunger . . .
Blessed are you who weep . . . " (Luke 6)

May we let these women touch us through the pages of this book and through the strength and weakness of their lives. And may our remembrance of Carla, Ita, and Maura always be a living memory. May we, with them, become the living memory of Jesus Christ in solidarity with the poor of our world.

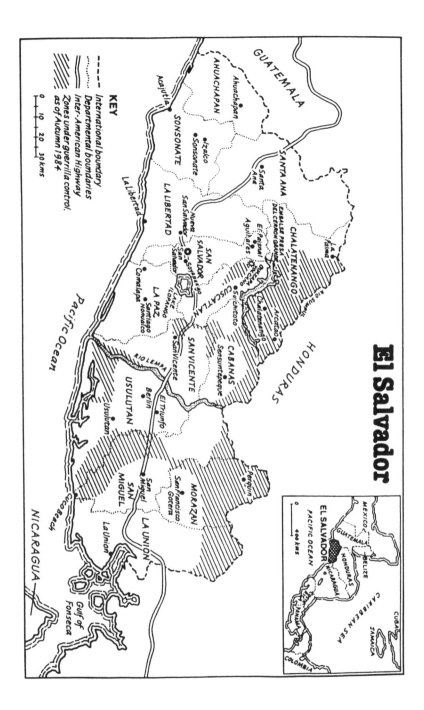

El Salvador

KEY

- International boundary
- Departmental boundaries
- Inter-American Highway
- Zones under guerrilla control, as of Autumn 1984

0   10   20   30 kms

GUATEMALA

HONDURAS

NICARAGUA

Pacific Ocean

AHUACHAPAN
Ahuachapán
SONSONATE
Izalco
Sonsonate
Acajutla
SANTA ANA
Santa Ana
LA LIBERTAD
Nueva San Salvador
San Salvador
SAN SALVADOR
Aguilares
El Paisnal
EMBALSE PRESA DEL CERRON GRANDE
CHALATENANGO
Chalatenango
La Palma
RIO LEMPA
Arcatao
CUSCATLAN
Suchitoto
CABAÑAS
Sensuntepeque
Soyapango
Lake Ilopango
LA PAZ
Santiago Nonualco
Comalapa
SAN VICENTE
San Vicente
RIO LEMPA
USULUTAN
Usulután
Berlin
El Triunfo
MORAZAN
San Francisco Gotera
SAN MIGUEL
San Miguel
Perquin
LA UNION
La Unión
Cojutepeque
Gulf of Fonseca
Rio Goascorán

PACIFIC OCEAN
MEXICO
GUATEMALA
BELIZE
EL SALVADOR
HONDURAS
NICARAGUA
CUBA
JAMAICA
CARIBBEAN SEA
PANAMA
COLOMBIA
0   400 kms

CHAPTER 1

A Common Grave

On Tuesday, December 2, 1980, with the annual meetings of their mission region concluded, the Maryknoll Sisters from Panama, Nicaragua, and El Salvador left the Diriamba Retreat House outside of Managua, Nicaragua, to return to their missions. Sisters Teresa Alexander, Madeline Dorsey, Maura Clarke, and Ita Ford were inconveniently booked on two separate flights to San Salvador, which would mean an extra round-trip to the airport for their friends, Ursuline Sister Dorothy Kazel and Lay Missioner Jean Donovan, who were picking them up.

At four o'clock, Madeline and Teresa arrived and were greeted by Dorothy and Jean, who assured them it would be no trouble to take them to La Libertad, where they had left their Jeep, and return later in the afternoon to meet Maura's and Ita's flight. A National Guardsman on duty in the airport watched the women and placed a phone call to his local commander.

It was after five o'clock when Madeline and Teresa drove away from La Libertad bound for their mission in Santa Ana and Dorothy and Jean climbed back into the white van to return to the airport. As they waited for Ita's and Maura's flight, which was one hour late and not due to arrive until seven, the National Guardsman placed another phone call. The local commander who took the call then ordered five guardsmen to change into civilian dress for an unspecified mission.

At around ten that night, along the old dusty road to San Pedro Nonualco, one hour from the airport and in the opposite direction from La Libertad, three peasants watched from a pineapple field as a white van drove by. It traveled another seven hundred yards and then stopped. The peasants heard machine-gun fire followed by single shots. Fifteen minutes later the same vehicle passed by on its way back. The lights inside were on, the radio blaring, and the peasants counted five bareheaded men. Later that night, the van was left burning on the side of the road leading from the airport to La Libertad.

Around seven-thirty the following morning, a peasant found the bodies of four North American women and informed the local judge who, by law, must identify bodies before burial. At eight-thirty, three members of the civil guard and two area commanders watched with the judge as four local residents dug a deep common grave in a fallow field behind barbed wire and pushed the bodies in.

Early in the morning of the next day, some peasants in the parish of San Vicente went quietly to tell their parish priest of the burial of four North American women. The administrator of the archdiocese of San Salvador, Bishop Rivera y Damas, was informed, and then United States Ambassador Robert White.

At noon on Thursday, December 4, Madeline and Teresa, Ambassador White, members of the missionary team from Cleveland, Ohio, and fifteen reporters watched as the bodies were unearthed and dragged, one by one, from the grave—first Jean, then Dorothy, Maura, and Ita.

The Sisters knelt to pray. Some of the reporters became ill. A few of the people who had gathered pulled at the long tough grass or looked for branches with which to cover the women.

On Friday afternoon, December 5, Bishop Rivera y Damas concelebrated the Mass of the Resurrection for the four women, followed by a wake which lasted throughout the night in La Libertad and at Asuncion in San Salvador.

On Saturday morning, December 6, Jean's and Dorothy's remains were accompanied to the airport for their respective flights to Sarasota, Florida, and Cleveland, Ohio, for burial.

The bodies of Maura and Ita were escorted by more than a dozen Jeeps, cars, and vans for the hot and potentially dangerous two and one-half hour trip to Chalatenango. There, only three months before, they had buried Sister Carla Piette, killed when a flash flood swept away the Jeep in which she and Ita had been traveling.

"We sang the same hymns," Madeline remembered, "and it was difficult to believe that Ita and Maura, who not so long ago had kept Carla's coffin from slipping too quickly down the muddy hill, were now being borne by us to be buried beside her in the little cemetery of Chalatenango, El Salvador."[1]

CHAPTER 2

Chile

Pushing Ita to safety the stormy night when she herself drowned was simply Carla's way of doing things: impulsively, completely, and well. The next day her broken, naked, lifeless body lay washed up on a sandbar in the El Zapote River.

When Carol Ann was born to James and Rose Piette in Appleton, Wisconsin, on September 29, 1939, she was more of a surprise than an afterthought, for two sons and a daughter were already grown. She adored her father, who loved her as well, and enjoyed nothing more than riding beside him in the front seat of his grocery's pick-up truck. When he died at home quite suddenly, her six-year-old heart ached with an intensity that would diminish in time but never completely subside. For the next several lonely years, she lived with her mother, whose grief and distance she, a child, could not understand.

When her sister, Betty, married a professional clown, Carol found him the most exciting person she had ever met. She loved Jack and for the rest of her life saw herself as a clown: the entertainer, the comic, the one with the big painted smile who cried often and bitterly beneath the mask.

Carol's lifelong friend Jackie Hansen Maggiore remembered:

> By the time we reached high school, Carol was quite tall, on the muscular side, with strong features, and dark curly hair. She was never a fashion plate or one to care about dress. She gave the appearance of being quite strong physically and emotionally; her vulnerabilities were a little more hidden. She had only a few close friends, but she was friendly and outgoing. Carol was always the class clown to some extent, never afraid to be outspoken and to challenge, making fun of Sister Placid's nervous habits and getting us all kicked out of

choir, challenging the young assistant pastor with, "How can you have a brand new car and skiing vacations and talk about poverty?" She was particularly fond of the common person and not at all impressed with snobs, whether social or intellectual.[1]

Midway into her freshman year at Marquette University, Carol read a pamphlet she had picked up in the back of church, noticed it was written by a professor on campus, and went immediately to speak with him. During the next few months Carol met several times with Father George Ganss, S.J., to discuss what had been set irreversibly in motion by his pamphlet, "On Thinking Out Vocations to Four States In Life." As in all things, Carol moved quickly and entered the Maryknoll Sisters the following September 1958. Her mother was opposed to Carol's decision and seemed to feel abandoned by her daughter.

Sister Rose Carol, as she was named on reception day, was "friendly, outgoing, jovial, bighearted and generous, but rather naive and tactless."[2] She eventually outgrew her naïveté, though the rest remained intact. Her joviality, which was to be an outstanding gift throughout her life, was not mere gaiety but a quick and sometimes painful grasp of the incongruous at the heart of even the most tragic happenings in life. This ability to comprehend a situation with such sensitivity, to distinguish the essential from the ridiculous and the arbitrary, was sometimes embarrassing, often bothersome, and later in life even dangerous. In the novitiate it was disconcerting when she was often unmercifully tickled by some archaic custom in the most silent and solemn of places and circumstances.

Though she shunned what was referred to as "intellectualism," she was in fact an outstanding student. As if having to put herself down, she made light of an art course "only open to hopeless cases" though she and one other Sister were the only survivors at the end of the term.

After completing her novitiate training and her college education—both with good grades and high recommendations—Carol was happy to be assigned to Chile in 1964. At the party given by the Sisters to welcome her in Santiago, it was Carla (as she would be called in Spanish) who delighted everyone with skits and songs.

The next day she cried lonely tears at the cold and strange impersonality of the Immigration Office.

Her rapid, unambiguous, and often flawed assessment of situations led her to strong convictions that she seldom hesitated to voice or act upon.

Even though she had only arrived in the country and hardly knew the Sisters, she was convinced that it would be far better for the community to study Scripture in the evenings than to pray the rosary, as was the custom. When the Sisters assembled in chapel after supper, the chairs had been rearranged, candles lit, the Bible opened, and readers assigned. Politely, awkwardly, the Sisters followed her lead, though for that one evening only.

Within a few weeks of her arrival in Chile, Carla waved good-bye to the women who would become her lifelong friends and boarded a train that took her south to language school in the picturesque country town of Pucon. Eight miles to the south a volcano reddened the clear night sky. Just a mile to the north was the large Villarica Lake surrounded by majestic pines. To the east the giant snow-capped Cordillera Range of the Andes Mountains pierced the heavens. And to the west stretched the long, white, lonely beach of the cold Pacific. Though the people of Pucon were warm and welcoming, the fruit and vegetables luscious and abundant, the community congenial, and the house comfortable, Carla soon became restless. She found the long mornings spent observing classes in the local parish school a waste of time, the Saturday mornings teaching English no challenge, and the two hours of repetition and stuttering conversation in the afternoons a frustration and a bore. All of this was intensified by a record eighty-five relentless days of winter cold and rain which depressed her. A childhood bronchial condition returned while she was in Pucon and would often recur as a hacking cough until the day she died.

But there was something else in Pucon that bothered her: the extreme poverty of the many and the equally extreme wealth of the very few. For the first time, she was aware of a chasm she could neither understand nor justify. Many of the children, even on the coldest day of the year, came to school without shoes. They lived with their brothers and sisters, parents, and often a grandparent or two in one-room, mud-floor wooden shacks. Their mothers earned about four dollars a month cleaning or cooking or baby-sitting in the large homes of the wealthy. Carla's journey with and toward the "poor ole beat-up people" had begun.

To the disappointment and dismay of her superiors, Carla ignored her textbooks and spent long hours reading and imitating the writings of Socialist poet Pablo Neruda and Nobel Prize winner Gabriela Mistral. On as many weekends as possible she would "escape the dark valley of tears" to go to the nearest Maryknoll Sisters house in Temuco to find some sun. There she met Sister Pat Cobb, from Jamaica, New York, who was a perfect match for Carla's spontaneity and often outrageous creativity. Together they painted the dreary bathroom, leaving daisies everywhere.

"Beat me to death with a wet noodle before I am forty,"[3] Carla would laugh, remembering her mother's age when she was born.

"Fifty-four sounds more reasonable to me," Pat decided.

In the end they agreed that whichever one survived would paint the other's coffin the colors of the rainbow.

Well before the year of language school was over, the regional superior, Sister Stephanie Kazmierczyk, originally from New Britain, Connecticut, decided to call Sister Mary Ellen Manz, the principal and superior in Chillan, from Jamaica, New York.

"Would it be all right if I sent Sister Carla Piette to you? Maybe you could break her in; she could do something in the school."

"Yes, that would be fine," Mary Ellen assured her, thinking in terms of the following week at the earliest. The very next morning, though it was raining quite hard, a smiling Carla knocked on the back door of the convent.

Carla had not been in Chillan very long before she announced that she intended to visit the office of the local four-page tabloid to tell them what she thought of their skimpy coverage of international news.

"You just arrived here," Mary Ellen pointed out, "and it is simply not fair to begin criticizing before you have a chance to understand. Just try to absorb for a year."

One year to the day, Carla said to Pat Cobb, who had since come to Chillan, "Well, today is the day!"

"What day?"

"The day we visit the newspaper."

After thanking the owner for his fine paper, Carla then told him, by the way, of the existence of special wire services that carry international news. He listened, delighted and somewhat amused, and then asked about their life and work. The following morning there appeared on the front page of the paper a picture of Carla and Pat along with a full-length feature article about these two kind Sisters who paid a visit and of the wonderful work they were doing in the parish and school of San Vicente.

During the next several years, Pat and Carla discovered much in common, including a sixth sense that alerted them to anything new or imminent, be it a circus, a concert, or a band of gypsies. There was another sense, too, which each knew the other had, though there was little need to speak of it: the sense of the tragic, the experience of an ache at the heart of life. In one area of interest, however, they disagreed so wholeheartedly that no amount of negotiating would help. Pat loved gardening, and wherever she went in Chile, she left flowers in well-tended plots.

"Come help me for an hour or so," Pat coaxed.

"I didn't come to Chile to pull weeds," Carla pointed out.

"Gardening can be very therapeutic," Mary Ellen tried to mediate.

"So can talking to people," Carla replied, and that was the end of it.[4]

When Carla arrived in Chile, the Church there and throughout the world was beginning to stir with the new insights of the Second Vatican Council. That the Church is of and for this world as well as for the next had been said perhaps more clearly than ever before. That here and now are to be the place and time for the beginning of the kingdom of God gave the Church an unequivocal mandate to preach and live the gospel of justice with love for the sake of peace.

In 1962 the National Episcopal Conference of Chile issued the document "Social and Political Responsibility in the Present Hour," which at that time was considered one of the most advanced positions taken by any Latin American Bishops Conference.

It put the Chilean Church solidly on the side of economic development, agrarian and other structural reforms, and a more equitable distribution of wealth. Cardinal Raul Silva of Santiago and Bishop Manuel Larrain of Talca turned over their dioceses' land to peasants for a pilot project in agrarian reform—a move promoted by both the Christian Democrats and the Marxists.

A palpable and well-founded fear of communism further fired the Church's dedication to social change. For far too long, Cardinal

Silva recognized, the Church had emphasized the sacraments and the education of the elite while nearly forgetting to teach the social doctrine of the Church. Now the communists were heralding what the Church had neglected to mention, and the hungry and oppressed were listening avidly.

Khrushchev was reported to have predicted that communism would enter Latin America by way of Chile. Indeed, most of the 270,000 declared communists of Latin America were already there and in control of the most powerful of the national syndicates, the Workers' Union. In 1958 the Communist Party had lost the presidential election by only 44,000 votes, a margin that was feared to be narrowing. While the Communist Party strove for victory at the polls in 1964, the Church set her hopes on Eduardo Frei Montalva, a Christian Democrat and former student of Bishop Larrain's in the social doctrine of the Church.

Cardinal Silva urged all Church personnel to make every possible effort, even at the cost of existing works, to reach the adult voting population. During the year 1963, thousands of priests, religious, and lay people touched virtually every Chilean home by way of house-to-house visits, neighborhood meetings, trips into distant rural areas, and radio programs. Though not consciously intended to be a political campaign, the Mission of 1963 certainly contributed to Frei's victory at the polls and to another communist defeat. The elections were over by the time Carla arrived, and the frenzied fear of communism had calmed as oppression, its fertile breeding ground, was being overcome.

Under Frei, community organizations were formed, women's groups were encouraged, farmers' loans were available, and a national campaign to educate the pueblo was launched. The problems were legion, of course; there were deep divisions and power plays, infighting and misuse of funds. But on the whole Chile breathed an air of promise.

Carla's letters at this time reflect the surge in society. She speaks of a sugar beet factory made possible by Alliance for Progress, a new local branch of the University of Chile, and increased tourism. But more significantly, her letters speak with sensitivity about the poor and with a growing awareness of her own poverty—themes which would develop throughout her life.

"I've seen so much misery and suffering that sometimes I walk home just repeating over and over, 'I believe, Lord, help my

unbelief,' " she wrote to her sister, Betty. "That poverty of spirit
that comes with the awareness of our own limitations is ever-present. God never ceases to teach us many things as we try to teach
others."[5]
In spite of her unorthodox ways, Carla was an excellent teacher.
When the school bell rang each morning, all of the 650 children of
San Vicente School, except Carla's, would line up in relative silence. "You shouldn't put kids in line. They should be free to go
into the classroom as they choose." Hers did precisely that, all
competing to be as close to Carla's towering figure as possible.
Within a short time, however, she came to understand what no one
could tell her: pandemonium is not creative.

There wasn't a student's home she didn't visit in order to know
the family or to understand why a child was tired or thin or bruised.
She would often rage at the parents' lack of concern or at the father's
drunkenness, but was never upset or impatient with the children.
In fact, it was remarkable how Carla was drawn always to the
slowest, the least attractive, the loneliest children as if there were
a special bond between them, an affinity which few could share.

Disheartened by the difficulty so many children had with reading, she searched and studied until she stumbled upon a fun
solution—regular classes in crawling to awaken the motor parts of
the brain. For an entire year she dedicated herself exclusively to
her "cement heads," as she called them with total affection. "We
crawled together and read together and eventually made some
slight progress," she reported proudly.[6]

No matter what problem might arise, Carla would attack it with
a burst of creative energy, enjoying the search for a unique solution.
When two of the Sisters came home with a bill for the lamp post
they had backed into, Carla slipped a forgotten silver-plated teapot
into her ever-present woven bag and went looking for a buyer. "You
can't be serious," she playfully bantered with one shop owner after
the other. "You know this fine antique is worth far more than the
pittance you are offering. Besides, my friends need $110."

In order to raise funds for a school project, she potted twenty-five
plants from Pat's garden and headed for the market. "Why, Madre
Carla," one of the women greeted her, "what are you doing?"

"I need some money for the school," she explained, arranging
her wares all around her on the ground as if she did it every day.
"Please just pray they last long enough to sell!"

At times Carla's uninhibited spontaneity was rather awkward and embarrassing for some of the Sisters. One such time was when the bishop came for his annual visitation. As son of the aristocracy and prince of the Church, the kind bishop was at ease with pomp and privilege. Carla cut through it with disarming familiarity. "My dear Sister Carla," the bishop was perfectly comfortable correcting her Spanish, "you do not use the familiar 'tu' with your bishop." "Why not?" she asked, with only a trace of challenge in her voice. He explained, as if to a child, all the while addressing her with "tu."

She was unmoved, however, and finally closed the subject when she asked, "You are my father, are you not, and children speak to their parents with 'tu'." The bishop became very fond of Carla.[7]

Throughout her life, Carla would have very little patience with what she considered clericalism in the Church, and often spoke of designing "Father formation programs" for the priests with whom she occasionally worked.

The years in Chillan were happy ones for Carla. On rare evenings without meetings, the Sisters would write letters, play cards, or sew and talk. It was always Carla's unique choice of words, her ability to capture a situation or a person with a delightful and insightful twist, that enlivened the conversation. She was especially famous for her nicknames. A very shy Father Brooker, who never said a word, was "Babbling Brooker." A rather stout Sister who was fond of the famous Chilean wine was "Jug Julie." Another Sister who loved nothing more than traveling and, amazingly, managed to do so, was dubbed "Pilgrim Princess." Inevitably those nicknames were received and used good-naturedly because they had been given with affection.

Carla was happy in Chillan but not without pain. The loosening of the structures of religious life in those post-Vatican II years allowed for greater personal responsibility and creativity, but it also caused turmoil and raised doubts about the future and even the validity of religious life.

Carla was not untouched by the rumblings and wrote of her confusion to Mother Mary Colman, "My heart is so full of searchings. I look for the road God points out but it's so foggy at times."[8]

And to her old friend Father Ganss she wrote, "It's impossible to judge anyone or their reasons for leaving, but it's so hard to see so many good friends taking off."[9]

Pat Cobb, more than anyone, helped her through those long months of doubt until she finally emerged confident of her vocation.

The Church of San Vicente in Chillan was packed with students and parents the night of her final vows. At that solemn moment when the priest raised the host, Carla was expected to approach and pronounce her vows. Instead, she walked to the microphone, motioned to the priest that she would be with him in a moment, and asked everyone to please be seated.

"What is she going to do now?" Mary Ellen whispered to Pat.

"I have no idea, but I wouldn't miss it for the world."

Carla simply had to speak what was in her heart. "Because I love God and Maryknoll and you, my dear, dear friends, I am able without wavering to promise to live as a Maryknoll Sister and to serve you until the day I die."

That in essence is what she said in Spanish, though there was more and a touch of poetry. Some eyes were not quite dry and the Sisters wanted to hug her then and there for that surprising and perfect moment.

In August 1971, after living seven years with Carla in Chillan, Pat returned to the States for four months of rest and renewal. Though nothing had been said, Carla sensed what was coming and wrote to Pat.

> This evening at Mass I had a strange experience. On my way to Church I felt great, rushing through the rain, trying hard to keep our silly dog Samba from dirtying my coat, and arrived in time to sing a duet with Brahms Brooker. As the Mass continued, and as the prayers were prayed, the Lord took my heart and tried to tell me something which I await to hear only from you. It was so real and yet I continue to ask Him for you and your happiness. What was it, friend? Why did I arrive home in tears? I say to myself, "I want her to be happy," and I really do. Yet I know I'll miss you terribly. Please tell me soon. No one saw me, only Samba.[10]

A month or two later, Pat wrote to tell Carla of her decision to leave Maryknoll, to stay in the United States, and to marry. Carla was hurt and lonely, and she prayed for a heart of stone. Less than a year later, Carla welcomed a change in assignment. "After seven years in Chillan," she wrote in May 1972, "and having lived in a fluctuating community of eight to six to three to five to two to six, I decided I should answer the Spirit and respond to the need in Buzeta where there were two Sisters alone with the school. So in March I dollied up to Buzeta here in Santiago."[11]

But Carla's restlessness did not abate in Buzeta. In fact it was further fired by a growing desire to live more closely with the poor. In many places throughout Latin America, and indeed the world, the Church's self-identity and understanding of its role in society was evolving away from institutions to community, from treating wounds to finding the source of society's sores, from a position of privilege and comfort to the enlightened place of serving with and for the marginated, the poor, and the oppressed. Carla wanted to be with the poor no longer as teacher, but in order to learn from them as neighbor, friend, and co-struggler. When Sisters Mary Tracy and Connie Pospisil indicated that they would like to have her join them in the *poblacion* ("shantytown") of La Bandera on the outskirts of Santiago, Carla needed no other incentive to move. Within a few weeks she was at home in La Bandera and wrote to her sister, Betty: "I love the work I am doing here. For the first time I feel as if I am living with the poor as I should be, that I am preaching the Good News to them as I should be, and that I am open to what the Lord sends today while trusting tomorrow to his hands."[12]

Within several months another Sister joined them, a Sister who had recently arrived from language school in Bolivia. Her name was Ita Ford.

CHAPTER 3

Searching

Ita Ford was only three years old the first time she left home. "Bye, Mom," she imitated her older brother Billy. "I'm going to school now." Usually, as the screen door banged behind her, Ita would settle down to play on the front steps of their red brick row house in Brooklyn. That day, however, when petite and attractive Mildred Ford went to retrieve her daughter, the porch was empty. After quickly checking with the neighbors and searching up and down the nearby streets, Ita's mother called the police. "Yes," they said to her relief, "we have your daughter." She had walked three long blocks and crossed two busy intersections before asking a kind woman who was sweeping her front walk, "Is this school?"[1]

Elaborate variations of the same theme would play throughout Ita Ford's life. She would go where she clearly knew she must, though she didn't always know the way. People would worry about her. But when she came back, sometimes bruised, she was far wiser than when she had left.

Ita's independent ways and penchant for wandering, far from giving the impression that she was detached or reckless, led one to realize that she was responsible and able to meet most obstacles with care and conviction. When she was only nine, Ita secretly went to the YWCA camp by subway instead of the slower but safer bus. When she told her parents at the end of the summer, they were impressed and thereafter entrusted their younger daughter René into Ita's care for the regular subway trip to visit their aunt in lower Manhattan.

Those free and responsible early years of Ita's life were not unprotected, however. Most of the children taught by the Sisters at Visitation Academy were middle class, full of gentle mischief, their innocence underexposed to life. Ita loved school and did quite well without being one-sidedly academic. In the eighth grade she

won the coveted General Excellence Medal and was faced with
having to give the first shaky speech of her life.

While Ita and René were in high school at Fontbonne Hall in
Brooklyn, their father had a relapse of tuberculosis and was forced
to retire from the insurance business. It was primarily from her
father that Ita received her polished gift of words and love of music.
His lovely tenor voice would harmonize with hers as they sat at the
kitchen table after school singing "Mandy, Mary," "Danny Boy,"
and all George M. Cohan's songs. Whenever Ita was traveling—to
Mexico, Russia, across the United States, to Bolivia and Chile—her
father would carefully weave long, eloquent and witty letters. She
saved them and took them, along with little else, to El Salvador.
But that was many years later.

On Saturday afternoons or when the evenings lingered long
enough, Ita and her lifelong friend, Grace Monahan, would ride
their bikes down to the Narrows, a particularly lovely and peaceful
area along Shore Road. There they would climb the railing and
snuggle into the familiar rocks for an hour or two to talk or quietly
listen to the sea gulls mew as the waves lapped against the shore.
It was there, in their high school years, that Ita sometimes spoke of
entering Maryknoll, the first North American Catholic foreign
mission community. She had never met her father's cousin,
Maryknoll Bishop Francis X. Ford, but remembered when he died
in a Chinese prison camp in 1952.

Though her dream was strong and clear, she was not in a hurry
to immediately live it. Her goal was so certain to come true that she
could live the intervening years without fear of losing it.

While studying literature at Marymount Manhattan College, Ita
spent vacations traveling with classmates Kate Monahan and Ana
May. In a cramped Volkswagon "bug," they ate hamburgers and
french fries and laughed all the way across North America and down
into Mexico. While staying at the least expensive and most interesting places along the way, they never hesitated to use the next-
door pool. Ita's "Peter Pan" shape and size and haircut puzzled a
ticket seller at Disneyland, who admitted her as Ana May's son.

In her senior year of college, Ita went on a student tour to Russia
and Poland, a trip that affected her deeply. Before leaving, she
wrote to Jean Rearden, a high school friend with whom she corresponded for the rest of her life. "I wrote to Maryknoll for application
after a warm-up letter," she said, "and today was answered with,

'Wait until you get back from your trip.' Maybe I can take my medical (exam) on graduation morning at the rate I'm going. Well, it's a short life and a merry one. . . . "[2]

The journey into Russia and Poland took Ita into a world more foreign than she had anticipated. The little bit of money she had changed in Poland went unspent—and therefore was relinquished at the border—because there was simply nothing to buy. The students with whom they spent an afternoon were delightful and gracious, but puzzled them with their one-sided view of world events. She was caught up in the euphoria of the parade to celebrate the Sputnik launch in Moscow and was saddened by the clamps put on people's freedom. But perhaps what affected Ita most deeply during the trip was the authenticity of religious expression in a country where religious belief was suppressed. On her return from Russia, Ita was more sure than ever of her vocation. "I think I have recently begun to know myself, and have re-evaluated a lot of things which used to seem so important to me," she wrote to Jean Rearden.

> For the first time in my life I am sure about what I want to do. You can't imagine what it was like being in Russia and feeling so impotent when people needed your help. A man next to me during a Russian Orthodox service cried during the whole Credo which the congregation chants. Religious barriers made no difference then—it no longer matters to whom one pledges allegiance, to the pope or patriarch—it was the idea that these people—the only ones I saw who really believed in God—not a lip service offering as my own is—but a soul-wrenching belief—the ones who really deserved freedom of religion—they were the ones denied it. It was pathetic and nauseating at the same time. I wanted so much to do something and couldn't. It was this—more than anything else in my life—which has made me aware now, that I really have to go to Maryknoll. I couldn't ever stay away after being in Russia.[3]

Several months later, in September 1961, Ita was one of sixty-four young women who arrived at the Maryknoll Sisters' Mother-house in Ossining, New York, to begin a year of postulancy. At first everything was simply new and different. She had not known any

of the women before; the motherhouse was strange and big; even
the quiet of the woods on that hill in Westchester County overlook-
ing the Hudson River was a far cry from Brooklyn. Eventually, some
of what was new and different became difficult. For the first time
in Ita's life, there were exact schedules and rigid rules dictating how
she was to live. And although virtually everyone did everything
together, close friendships were frowned upon as potential distractions to one's relationship to God. She was lonely and wrote of that
loneliness to Jean only weeks after their arrival, when some of the
women had already gone home.

> As for the group around me, there are fifty-nine very different
> people. I know them all and not at all. For the next three years
> it's not allowed to recreate in two's and it's impossible to
> communicate mob-style. The ages range from eighteen to
> thirty-two; no one is very offensive and there are many affable
> ones. . . . It's lonely. Not in the sense of being alone in a crowd
> but in an emotional way. No one knows you well enough to
> be able to say the right thing when you need it and as yet no
> one cares enough. I miss many people, some much more than
> others. This is sheer institution, because of the large group,
> and I hate this phase of it, to the point that when I thought
> I'd climb a wall I expected to see everyone else there too.[4]

Ita recognized that she was generating much of her own frustration and concluded evenly, "My whole problem, one that's plagued
me my whole life, is impatience. I expect to conquer everything in
one try and with one look. You don't do that with a new life."[5]

Second only to loneliness and discomfort with crowds, intellectual boredom bothered Ita. "School-wise the only thing new is
Gregorian chant. I get very bored because most of the classes seem
repetitious and ridiculous."[6]

But her sense of humor carried her through. "Thursday night is
confession night and every week I resist the impulse to go in and
say, 'Bless me, Father, I'm a saint.' But tonight, as I was gabbing
away, the priest said I could have the *New Yorker* after I've digested
all of St. Paul's epistles to the point of application!"[7]

As the months moved on into a year and then two and the women
moved to the East Coast Novitiate in Topsfield, Massachusetts,
Ita's attitudes and reactions matured until she genuinely came to

appreciate what had bothered her before. Looking back on her frustration with the relative lack of intellectual stimulation, she wrote:

> The first weeks I thought my brain might deteriorate if I couldn't have access to the 800's of the Dewey decimal system. I thought a few books wouldn't break me, that the *New Yorker* would be nice, and that I was starved for news. Now, you could answer, that they've succeeded in making me happy living in a vacuum. No, not at all. There's a substitution—not a tit for tat, not the *Tablet* for the *Times*— rather it's an inside yourself deal. You spend more time trying to understand.[8]

To her surprise, she found that she could and did love "a whole roomful of people."

> There is so much I feel now, that I never let myself before. For the first time—and it's bizarre that it should happen here—I'm allowing myself to love and be loved. It's a matter of being involved with everyone to a certain point because you can't give yourself to one person. I never thought I could look at a whole roomful of people and honestly say I love them all. I can't explain it. I do.[9]

As each month passed, Ita seemed to be entering into her new life with greater peace and conviction.

> I'm not a fan of much of the symbolism attached to religious life. But there is a definite relationship to be established with God, and maybe with less sentiment it could be clearer. It's joy, it's peace. It's wonderful to be called. It's dizzying to know you're loved so. Just to have the knowledge of the love that exists, and the reality of the relationship you can have with God—something I am at a complete loss as to how to explain to anyone who thinks this is a waste of time.
>
> I guess I finally committed myself. I sort of realize I can only be myself by doing it. Even if it means being a mediocre clod, I've got to be one now, here. It's a little like the "Hound of Heaven"—you run right smack into God. And in the

beginning it's elation. Then you realize what it means. It's
good I don't know it all now, but only a little because it would
be crushing—especially because I can no longer chuck it.[10]

In January 1964 the young women who remained with Ita in the
novitiate at Topsfield were looking forward to June, when they
would make their first vows. "It's going to be hard around Easter,"
Ita wrote, "when the Council votes again [on who will be allowed
to profess her vows as a Maryknoll Sister and who must leave]. If it
hurt to see them go when we were postulants, two more years of
being together doesn't make it easier."[11]

"We're here until the end of June," Ita wrote to Jean in April.
"Profession is the 24th with eight days of retreat before it." And
then, as if hinting of something else, she ends, "This isn't a
sparkling letter by a long shot. I'm a little down in the mouth right
now, but I'm sure it will right itself soon."[12]

For several months Ita had not been well. Julie Miller, from
Savannah, Georgia, tried to help her hide the frequent bouts of
nausea from their superiors. Eventually, her condition became
apparent and she was sent to the doctor. In June, with less than two
weeks to go before the novices were to make their vows, Ita wrote,

> My stomach has been on the skids, and last Monday the
> doctor asked that I not be under the pressure of taking vows
> on the 24th. The Mother General said all right, so it looks as
> if I'll be summering in Massachusetts. René and Bill's wife,
> Mary Ann, are flying up tomorrow, mostly to put everyone's
> mind at ease that I really needed a little time to ease off the
> pressure.[13]

On August 15, 1964, Ita wrote the last lines of this chapter of her
life.

> I'm home. Wednesday afternoon it was official that I couldn't
> take vows. I didn't want to shock you by calling up or ringing
> the bell. René's baby will be due within the week but I'll call
> Tuesday or Wednesday after I know you've gotten this. It's
> a shock and a disappointment and I don't think I'm operating
> on all engines but I'll bounce soon.[14]

The next few months were difficult. Ita could not understand what happened or why. "Why?" would always be the unanswerable question she always asked when life seemed cruel. How she envied René and Bill's wife, Mary Ann, for having their life decisions behind them. She spent long hours listening to Julie Miller's piano recordings and talked as if puzzled about what had happened. But she was never bitter, only baffled and wounded. For a while she commuted to Boston to continue to see the doctor there until she knew it was no longer necessary. "I'm going out for a walk," she told her mother one day. When she returned she announced, "I smiled at everyone I met. Some smiled back."[15]

"It takes time getting back into things which are different, if not diametrically opposed to the way I've been thinking for the past three years," Ita wrote to her former novice mistress, with whom she would remain good friends. "But the graces keep coming, so I'm confident it will all work out."[16]

Within a month of her dismissal from Maryknoll, Ita enrolled in several courses in the Education Department of Hunter College. She was teaching catechism to Puerto Rican junior-high-school students not far from Chinatown, reading for the blind, and working full time as an editor of high-school English and religion texts with Sadlier Publishing Company in New York City.

Most of the editors of Sadlier's Religion Department were young and unmarried. They were a group of liberal Catholics who worked together, partied together, and protested the war in Vietnam. Ita was very much at the center of that. They went to Washington for rallies and civil rights marches and wrote letters to Congress. On the wall of her apartment in Sheridan Square was a poster that said, "What if they gave a war and nobody came?"

These were important years for Ita, years of growing and defining. By choice she lived simply, centering on essentials, and often said how precious life is and not to be squandered in distractions. Above all, friends were central to her life.

In the evenings she and her roommate, Kate Monahan, her friend from college days, would read, talk, or wander with friends to Greenwich Village. Occasionally they would buy standing-room-only tickets for the opera or theater. Admission to their Christmas party was one handmade ornament per guest.

In dress, Ita was just as unelaborate. Ana May remembers meeting Kate and Ita for supper at Alice's Place from time to time.

There she was in the same outfit—always neat, always meticulous, but never the chic lady she could have been. She wasn't into that. She was very pretty, naturally pretty, and never used any makeup at all. She had a raincoat, her penny loafers, and a few wool sweaters that she wore for years.[17]

As an editor, Ita was highly respected and depended upon for her compassionate and critical mind. She would move material around and add what was missing with such sensitivity and respect for the author that they always became good friends.

Both in writing and in conversation, Ita chose her words carefully, never saying more than she meant. This attentiveness to precision ultimately produced papers and letters that are a joy to read. In conversation, however, her deliberate care with words resulted in groping, sometimes mumbling speech that increased in direct proportion to the importance of the topic. It was particularly exasperating to talk to Ita by phone, for her tendency was to swallow the last two words of every sentence. But how she loved to talk, to spend long hours traveling through literature, theology, politics, the theater. Though she often became excited about an issue or an idea, she would never outshout or interrupt. She would patiently wait her turn, listening, and then contribute something usually more insightful and wittier than what had been said so far. It was this—her listening stance toward life, her sensitivity to situations and moods, her need to understand and hesitancy to judge, her ability to accept precisely who a person was and what she was saying—that accounted for Ita's extraordinary and extensive gift of friendship.

During her Sadlier years she met a young Japanese-American lawyer whose family had been interned on the West Coast during World War II. Ita dreamed of a large family and a quiet home in a rural area. Yet the longer they spoke of marriage, the more persistent her older dream became.

In a sense it is true to say that Ita never left Maryknoll, for the contact was never broken. She regularly corresponded with a number of friends who were by then in Africa, Latin America, and the Orient, and her decision to move into an apartment was prompted by the constant stream of Maryknoll friends wanting to see her in the city.

In the summer of 1970, Ita joined a tour going to Japan, where Julie Miller had been assigned the year before. For two wonderful weeks they traveled and talked. Finally, the day before she was to leave, Ita mentioned what was uppermost in her mind.[18] "What do you think of my entering Maryknoll again?" The next morning she caught up with the tour she had never been with and waved good-bye, smiling. The following summer she called Tokyo to tell Julie she was off to the Maryknoll Sisters' Formation House in St. Louis, Missouri.

CHAPTER 4

State of Siege

Religious life had changed in the seven years since Ita had left Topsfield. In contrast to the rambling institutional novitiate Ita had disliked, the formation house in St. Louis was a large family home like that of their neighbors in the midtown section of the city. Ita was one of three young career women who entered the Maryknoll Sisters that year, a relief from the "mob" she had found it difficult to relate to years before. The many rules that had defined and directed religious life had evolved into participation by the members of the community in deciding their times of prayer, study, work, and recreation.

In almost ludicrous contrast to Ita's pining away after the "800s of the Dewey decimal system" in 1961, her letters in 1971 and 1972 were full of good-natured complaints about the amount of work generated by their classes at St. Louis University.

"Sorry it has taken me so long to answer your notes," she wrote to Jean Rearden Baumann. "Sabbatical year is a little busier than I had anticipated. Between Scripture courses at the divinity school and theology here at the house, work has been piling up. I'm at a slight disadvantage not knowing Greek, German, Hebrew, but I admire it on the pages. Greek is especially graceful!"[1]

Though religious life had changed, Ita did not see herself as markedly different from the young woman she had been seven years before. She wrote of the past and the present:

After a month I can say I'm glad I'm here. It's strange to realize that I'm back again going toward what I want. And I may have a case of arrested development, but sometimes I feel as if I've been through it before. In a sense I feel like I'm back home. Of course it's different and I am too, and I expected that, but sometimes, when praying or free-associating, I have the feeling that my heart is moving or being moved as it may have eight years ago. Either I'm very consistent or I'm still in the same place I was then.[2]

In the spring of 1972 Ita was surprised to be told that "considering that I had already fulfilled canonical requirements [at Topsfield] I could make what is now called a promise of fidelity. After considering it for a while— because I hadn't been expecting to do it for at least another year—I've decided to do it before I leave St. Louis."[3]

Ita and the other two women in her group had been considering the mission countries in which they might best be able to serve. "Next year you may find me in Chile or the Philippines," she wrote. "Last week Korea was also on the list, but the first two have large pastoral institutes that develop catechetical materials for the surrounding areas and with my experience, I probably could get involved in some aspect of that. However, I won't be doing anything until I get a grasp of the language."[4]

Ita was assigned to Chile following six months of language school in Bolivia. Stopping in several places in Central America and Peru on her way to Cochabamba, Bolivia, in August 1972, she saw things about which she had only read and heard. She saw the blatant wealth of the few and smelled the poverty of the masses and was amazed at how casually and blindly they seemed to live side by side. In Lima, Peru, she went from the colonial presidential palace at the center of the capital city to the latest of the many "invasion sites" on the outskirts. There she saw the squalor in which tens of thousands of rural people live without water, without light, without roads, in the cardboard boxes they have for homes. "It struck me as I kept seeing things I had only heard about that I wasn't reacting to it. I was only seeing and not understanding. There's so much incongruity that it's very hard to get hold of it. A person would have to be here a long time before beginning to understand."[5]

For the next six months, on the edge of the quaint and colorful city of Cochabamba, Ita "twitched" through five hours of Spanish conversation a day. Though impatient to be perfect, she was good-naturedly so. "I'm looking forward to the time when I get out of the one-word-at-a-time-with-a-big-pause-in-between-phase. At this stage, if the person listening to me hasn't forgotten what I started to say, I probably have."[6]

As her tongue twisted around the new language, so her mind wrestled with events.

Last Thursday Bolivia was declared in a "state of siege," which best translates to being under martial law, a not-un-common occurrence in these parts. It is just about a month since the currency was devalued sixty percent causing suffering for most of the people. Last week two unions in La Paz had the temerity to consider striking as a protest to the economic situation, and out rolled the tanks. Things have been quiet here in Cochabamba, but the decree is for the entire country—no meetings, no travel within the country without permission, no more than three people together on the street at night, etc. But life seems to go on.[7]

Language studies completed, Ita was ready to go to Chile.

Yes, I'm about to move. I'm flying to Santiago on Wednesday, March 14. To what and where I still don't know. I'm presuming that it will all gradually work out. Being in South America, I'm learning to live with a lot of unknown factors.

In a sense Wednesday is a big leap into the unknown. But it's one that I should make now. I don't know what it holds or what it really means, but with all the uncertainty, it still seems to sit right. This life is certainly crazy in some aspects. Just when you begin to feel comfortable, you uproot. I've met some fine people here, so I presume there will be others along the way. That doesn't take the edge off saying good-bye, but it certainly is good to know some of the people spread around who are involved in the same effort as yourself, who share the same hope. In that way the transiency is worth it.[8]

In the middle of March, with one suitcase, her books, and a duffel bag full of paper products that had been unavailable in Chile for some time, Ita arrived in Santiago to begin what she thought would be only one month of becoming acquainted with the country, the Sisters, and their works before settling down. But at the end of May, two and one-half months later, Ita was still

roaming, supposedly getting some brief idea of what is going

on and how Maryknoll is relating to it. I think what happened
was that I just got very confused and tired. Some people say
I couldn't have come at a more exciting time, while others say
this is a terrible introduction. I guess that's indicative of
what's going on.[9]

Ita didn't know it then—in fact, few people did—but she had
entered a country whose democratically elected socialist government was being ruthlessly undermined. Even before Salvador
Allende was elected in March 1970, strong internal and external
forces were at work to counter the socialist experiment of Eduardo
Frei.

When Eduardo Frei Montalva was elected by an absolute majority in September 1964, Chile's chronic social problems—poverty, hunger, malnutrition, and lack of real representation for the
poor—were being felt more and more in the urban centers. Rural
peasants were crowded into urban slums, and problems in housing,
employment, just wages, and decent working conditions were
increasing. The series of reforms that Frei instituted did not resolve
the economic and social difficulties, and different political parties
in Chile became increasingly polarized in their solutions to Chile's
woes. Even within Frei's Christian Democrat Party, there were
sharp divisions.

When Frei was unable to succeed himself as president in 1970,
his divided party chose Radomiro Tomic as the Christian Democrat
candidate. In the meantime, Allende and the Socialists were again
making a strong bid for the presidency. Not only were the Christian
Democrats and the right-wing parties of Chile worried about an
Allende victory, but United States President Richard Nixon and
Secretary of State Henry Kissinger were determined to do everything within their power to prevent a Socialist Party triumph.

When Allende was elected, important Chilean political and
business leaders swore they would do everything they could to
subvert his "experiment." The financial and moral backing of the
Nixon administration greatly increased their leverage. Forces were
unleashed that ultimately resulted in the breakdown of Chile's
political system.

For several months prior to Ita's arrival in Santiago, people had
been banding together in different areas of the city to stop black-
market trading and ensure that the available goods were fairly

distributed. By enrolling, residents were entitled to buy goods according to the size of their family. The long-standing shortages of machine parts and vital consumer goods touched nearly everyone, including the upper classes, who had never been accustomed to scarcity. Former President Frei's wife initiated the "saucepan marches" made up of hundreds and then thousands of housewives who clanged lids against metal pots in order to protest the shortage of meat, sugar, coffee, rice, fish, cooking oil, detergent, toothpaste, soap, toilet paper, and noodles. When the flour mills went on strike in August, it was necessary to stand in line for half a day to buy a single loaf of bread. The truckers' strike was the straw that finally broke the country's back. Not even Mrs. Frei knew that the United States had sent $8 million to insure its success.

But in spite of the troubled atmosphere, the people, to Ita's surprise, were less than gloomy. "There's an incredible adaptability to the circumstances and a great sense of humor. I must say I'm learning all kinds of lessons about where you put priorities and just what are some of the basic pleasures of life."[10]

In June, the middle of winter, Ita spent several weeks with a Chilean Sister who was working in *Poblacion Manuel Rodriguez* "principally for immersion in the language." The area was

one of Santiago's innumerable *poblaciones* which I guess could be described as resettlement areas—or areas which just become inhabited by people squatting on unused property. From beginnings in tents or a one-room wooden affair, there gradually is construction of small individual homes. I would guess there are about 5,000 families here—and maybe a third have a permanent home—usually wood or brick, small, considering the size of the families, but a source of real pride.

This gives me some idea of *poblacion* work, of which there is much now, since the movement is away from institutions and toward living with the people in their reality, working toward forming community among small local groups. It's a far cry from Sheridan Square—but comfortable enough, now that I'm getting the knack of knowing how many layers of clothes I need to keep warm.

Where I'll be in July or so I still don't know. I'm drawn to Santiago as a place—probably because my blood is urban.

> Wherever it is, I hope to unpack for a while. There are times
> when the image of pilgrim Church gets to be a little too real![11]

By the end of July, Ita had decided to accept the invitation to
join three Maryknoll Sisters who lived in the *poblacion* La Bandera—Mary Tracy, originally from Evergreen Park, Illinois, Connie
Pospisil from New York City, and Carla Piette. "Two of the three,
Connie and Carla, are recent arrivals," Ita wrote, "so it's somewhat
like a new beginning. Home is a small wooden house with three
bedrooms and a one-room living-dining-kitchen. Also indoor
plumbing. It's comfortable and simple."[12]

Several weeks after moving in, in September 1973, Ita and Carla
went to Talca, a few hours away by bus, for a weekend workshop.
That Sunday morning, September 10, Ita's brother Bill finally got
through by phone from New York to the Maryknoll Sisters' Center
House in Santiago and left the message that was carried to La
Bandera. Connie called Ita from the parish phone, several blocks
away. "Ita, Bill called this morning to say that your dad died. Ita,
I'm sorry, are you ok? They want you to go home."

Father Tom Maney drove Ita and Carla to Santiago that afternoon. "I just don't know," Ita thought out loud with the Sisters. "If
Dad were still alive, there would be no question, but I'm just
beginning to unpack my bags and to understand what is going on
in this crazy country and it's time to move again."

"If you don't want to go, don't go." Connie tried to offer her
support while preparing supper in the kitchen. In the end, the
combined voices of everyone else persuaded her. But it was Carla
more than anyone who urged her to go, for though it was many years
earlier, she still resented having been "protected" from the sight of
her father in death and not having been allowed to attend his
funeral.[13]

The next morning, Monday, September 11, 1973, Ita stayed
home to pack while Carla and Father Maney drove into Santiago
to arrange for a ticket on the next flight to New York. Near the
center of the city, traffic was being detoured away from the main
plaza and Carla sensed that people were upset or afraid. She turned
on the radio and they listened as President Allende told of an
uprising in Valparaiso earlier that morning. That was a hundred
miles away. Father Maney parked his truck and they began to walk
to the Braniff office, several blocks away. Soon there were tanks,

and then the Hawker Hunter fighter planes began to fly low overhead. Crouching, Carla and Father Maney ran back to the truck and returned to La Bandera.

Though the Chilean people were unarmed, the presidential palace and the surrounding center of the city were bombed as if to give the impression that a massive uprising had been the provocation for the coup, which was in fact a massacre. By mid-afternoon Allende was dead, his ministers in prison and the entire country tightly under military rule. Workers rushed home through the empty streets, knowing they would be shot if they were not indoors by six o'clock. Anybody caught conversing on the street would be arrested. The radio played martial music and barked orders. "Workers go home quickly, no loitering."

Then came the long list of the junta's alleged enemies: ministers, lawyers, doctors, and university professors were to present themselves to the authorities. Tanks and trucks full of soldiers and shiny new cars with high-ranking military officials were the only signs of life on the streets. Raids were made on the *poblaciones* and hundreds of men, women, and children were either killed or taken prisoner. Only much later did the Sisters learn of the aborted plan to bomb La Bandera. The grief-stricken wife of one of the military men who sabotaged the planes and was subsequently executed whispered that story to the Sisters.

On September 13 the curfew was lifted from noon to three. Miraculously, the supermarkets that had long been empty were overflowing with previously hidden staples, far too expensive now for anyone but the rich.

Chile was sealed in a state of siege that allowed the rest of the world to know very little for the next ten days. During this time as many as 30,000 people are believed to have been killed.

"Now it is more important than ever that you go," the Sisters told Ita. "You have to tell people what is happening down here."[14] Day after day Ita and Carla's nerves were tested as they went from one government office to the next in the war-pocked center of town, trying to get the necessary travel papers. Everywhere they were met by machine guns and angry men standing guard over the confusion. Finally, on September 21, the Sisters drove Ita to the barricade about one mile from the airport, where she boarded a bus that would take her to the first plane leaving the country since the morning of September 11.

Though Ita did her best to tell people what she had seen and heard and felt during the coup, many of her friends were politely incredulous when she mentioned United States involvement. They saw her trembling and feared she might have been strained beyond her limits.

After several weeks in New York and the promise of a visit from her mother, Ita was happy to "go home" to Chile and her friends.

CHAPTER 5

Carla and Ita

Within a few short weeks, Carla and Ita had become good friends. Ita's passion for a clear and many-sided view of things left her open to receive and fairly evaluate a wide variety of opinions and attitudes—even Carla's abrasive ones, which often irritated others. Carla's tendency to react impulsively was held in check by Ita's need to analyze, just as Ita's hesitancy to act until everything was clear was pushed along by Carla's need to move. They simply fit.

They both devoured books and loved discussing them, often long into the night when they were at their best and everyone else had gone to bed. Carla's penchant for puns and inventiveness with words and phrases delighted Ita, who truly appreciated, sometimes criticized, and almost always understood what Carla said through her poetry. They were opposite and alike. Carla was outgoing, boisterous, argumentative, large in size and presence. Ita was retiring, unimposing, listening, petite. They made an incongruous pair. But what they shared most deeply was a seriousness about life that touched humor and felt pain and was impatient with anything less than the truth or contrary to the kingdom of God. Their love for the people of La Bandera was something else they shared.

To a visitor, La Bandera was the most depressing of the *poblaciones* that skirted Santiago. Though perhaps no poorer or more crowded than the other *poblaciones*, the people of La Bandera seemed tougher, and their tight little dusty wooden houses seemed to go on and on forever.

Merchants, construction workers, maids, housekeepers, and thieves, most of the 80,000 inhabitants had only a grade-school education or less. They had come from the country or smaller towns believing that a less-hungry future would be found in the city. Anger lived on the surface of life, and understandably so, for they had legitimately tried to find a better life, only to be cornered at every turn. Most of the men and many of the women drank too much of the cheap Chilean wine to forget their pain or to remember joy.

But the Sisters never saw Bandera as ugly or as an exceptionally tough place in which to live. Their house was burglarized only once, and that was an "innocent burglary," they said. It happened when some young men went to the house looking for Connie to care for a wounded friend. Finding no one home, they angrily kicked the door, which opened easily. They walked in, finding little more to take than small appliances and an alarm clock in each of the rooms but Carla's. Ever since she was small, she had counted on her father to wake her up, and he always did.

One night a stranger knocked at the door. Carla was up as usual. "Let me in!" he whispered anxiously. "The soldiers are after me." They sat in the dim light and talked for over an hour until it was safe for him to leave.

"What work do you do?" Carla asked, making conversation.

"I steal for a living," he replied. These were the people she loved, the "poor ole beat-up people" of La Bandera.

In many respects their life was lived in a fishbowl. Everyone knew who was visiting, when they came and left, and often what they talked about. Nothing was secret, everything was shared, for hospitality was and remains the central and most famous characteristic of the Chilean people.

It took some time for everyone to become accustomed to the fact that these Sisters did not have clothes to give away or money to lend or medicines to dispense. "We don't have a big warehouse," Ita was always saying, "but perhaps together, with all of our neighbors who have the same problem, we can find a solution for all." When several families lost everything but their lives in a raging fire, the neighbors met to distribute whatever clothing, food, and household articles that could be spared.

"We counted on their spirit of sharing," Carla wrote after the fire, "and they responded beautifully. Each one was saying to the other, 'Try these' or 'Don't these fit your little girl?' or 'These would be good for Jose's baby.' I continue to learn from our gorgeous people. I look at my values of security, cemented in me by years of thrift and hard work at getting ahead, and lay them next to the values I see here. It seems to me that the Christian way of sharing can only become a reality within the surroundings of the poor."[1]

To the left of the Sisters' house, only feet away, was the local bar. The head of Ita's bed was about five feet from that of the couple next door. "You're into the fights, you're into the joys, you're into the disagreements, into the struggle," she explained.[2]

There were no such things as office hours. Any time of the night or day a crisis might arise—a sick neighbor, someone missing, a friend just wanting to talk. Ita was in bed one afternoon battling bronchitis when she heard a knock but decided to ignore it. "Hey, Ita," the women called, "we know you're in there." After several stones were rolled down the roof, she finally got up and went to the door.

"Hi, Ita," they said. "We just came by to see how you're feeling."

Though life would never return to normal after the coup, daily routines were more or less resumed. Carla continued to commute to Buzeta, where she taught until the end of the year, and met with the women's prayer group. Since the military takeover, Carla had to fight with strong discomfort each time she met with these women, who were largely Chilean Air Force wives. She wrote to her sister, Betty:

Our people have suffered so much and our house has been searched twice. You can't walk down the streets without meeting a pointed loaded machine gun in the hands of the ever-present military. However, I know they are people, too—in fact I have a group of mothers, in another section of Santiago, whose husbands are in the service. They are also Christians and I believe that if someone doesn't work with them, "How will they know?" as St. Paul says.[3]

Carla quickly became good friends with a number of the Air Force wives, particularly with Nalda, whose husband suffered a nervous breakdown as a result of having to torture his own people.

There were so many people desperately looking for help in finding their disappeared and imprisoned family members and friends that the Lutheran, Catholic, and Jewish communities founded the Ecumenical Committee for Peace for that purpose. The scope of the work quickly expanded to deal with the unemployed and the hungry as well. Nationwide, a campaign was launched to feed 30,000 children each day with funds donated by international agencies and local merchants. Once a week Carla and Ita would make the rounds of the stores soliciting contributions for the five local *comedores* (dining rooms) where the mothers took turns cooking for 400 children. Though the *comedores* would be a constant source of frustration for Carla for the next several years, she nonetheless delighted in how much she learned. Exasperated by a mother who repeatedly failed to acquire the birth certificate necessary to enroll her children in the program, Carla finally said to her, "Señora Rosa, if you do not register your children, their places in the dining room will be given to someone else."

> I was blind to her undernourished state, which leaves one more than somewhat apathetic. That evening some other mothers came to me: "Carla, you are always saying that the right to eat comes from God. How can you take away that right just because someone doesn't do what you want her to do?"
>
> That simple statement of profound truth, spoken in friendship and sincerity, taught me volumes. They were right, very right, and I was very wrong. It is humbling and joyful to know that evangelization is going on within the Church. I have come to see that among the poor with whom I have come to share my life, I am perhaps one of the poorest. Of the oppressed to whom I have been sent to teach liberation, perhaps I am the most oppressed. And learning this, I'd say I've learned a lot.[4]

In fact, the entire Church was learning a lot in those days. In 1963, the Chilean Church could not have known where it was going or what it would find when it approached the poor. Though it was in no small measure a fear of communism that made Church personnel go to the poor, they stayed with them because they came to recognize the legitimacy and importance of a struggle to give birth to a just society, a society more consistent with the kingdom of God. Paradoxically, that birth seemed most imminent in the midst of the brutal attempt to prevent it. Ita expressed a sense of that birth in an interview in 1978.

> What is important to me is creating or building the kingdom [of God], trying to understand just what the future might be

if there really were bread for all the people, if there really were
justice, and if I cared enough to put myself there. It really
seems more urgent in some parts of the world than in others.
The kingdom is there and not there at the same time because
in the middle of the oppression or the sinful structure, the
reaction to that is the beginning of the kingdom. I don't feel
comfortable there. There are a lot of things that are very
uncomfortable about being there, but it is the right place to
be. It's as if you intuit a place—this is your place right now. I
can't say it's my place for ever and ever. Right now, I recognize this is where I should be. It's not the most comfortable
place in the world.[5]

In their meetings in Medellín, Colombia, in 1968 (and later even
more strongly in Puebla, Mexico, in 1979) the Latin American
bishops spoke of what Ita referred to as "not the most comfortable
place in the world." They were overwhelmed, in fact, by the
horribly unjust, inhuman conditions in which the vast majority of
the Latin American people were forced to live. "The misery that
besets large masses of human beings in all of our countries," the
bishops said, "expresses itself as an injustice which cries to the
heavens."[6]

They spoke of the poverty of the masses and of their repression
as a "situation of sin," particularly scandalous on a Catholic continent. They blamed the upper classes and foreign monopolies who
represent an "international imperialism of money" for the "institutionalized violence against the overwhelming majority of the Latin
American people who yearn for liberation from all servitude."[7] The
means of liberation varied as diverse groups searched for solutions.

To the chagrin of the Chilean hierarchy, "Christians for Socialism" was founded by 80 priests during the Allende years in order
to dialogue with the Marxists in an attempt to find a gospel-based
alternative to communism and capitalism. The group grew quickly
to include thousands of members in 19 countries in Europe and
America. On the far right, meanwhile, were Catholic splinter
groups such as the "Society for the Defense of Tradition, Property,
and Family," which was actively engaged in resistance to Allende
both inside and outside institutional politics. When the military
took power from Allende in 1973, most of the members of Christians for Socialism were expelled or harassed, and many lay people,

priests, and religious were persecuted if known to be working for social change. In a letter written in November 1974, Ita mentions only one incident in the growing Church-State tension.

> Last week arms were planted in a tabernacle in a small chapel in the same section of Santiago as we are. The priest was taken on the charge of aiding the extremists. So it continues, but the Church is taking a stand. Within a day and a half a pastoral letter was sent out, denouncing the whole incident as a put-up.
>
> The tension between Church and State helps keep us all honest. You have to make decisions, even though they won't be popular and can easily be twisted. So we muddle along ...[8]

The repression by the military against the pueblo's antipathy to military rule would continue far longer than anyone dreamed. Every night, as soon as curfew fell, the shots began—shots that may have signaled someone's death or were intended to terrify.

By day there was fear as well, fear of the unreasonable and arbitrary behavior of those in power, against which there was virtually no recourse. A priest neighbor of the Sisters who taught a course in Marxism in the political science department of the Catholic University was expelled after the coup. In the terror of those first days before it was clear that the priest would have to leave the country, he buried his textbooks in his yard. Several months later the new owners of the house went to the Sisters to say that the family living in the adjacent house was adding a room and had begun to dig in the direction of the buried books. They were afraid of reprisals if subversive materials were found on their property.

"Early Sunday morning, when no one is awake, dig them up and bring them over here in a wheelbarrow," Sister Connie Pospisil told them. "Then we'll figure out what to do with them."

"It was crazy," Connie admits in hindsight, "but they were perfectly good textbooks and we hated to burn them. We burned the papers but hung the books all over the house to dry and then put them in a suitcase way in the back of the closet shelf."[9]

Several weeks later, the Sisters' house was searched for the third time. The first time it had been searched by the army, the second time by the air force, but this time it was the more professional plainclothes police who came.

There was no knock, only the sudden crash of the door against the wall as they burst in, six of them with guns ready.

"Up against the wall; hands up!" While three men aimed their guns at Ita, Carla, and Mary Tracy, the other three ransacked the little house. They quickly went from room to room, not searching so much as simply upsetting everything. They emptied drawers on the floor, overturned mattresses, toppled bookshelves. Even if there was nothing to find, they always "discovered" something if their intent was to intimidate or to arrest.

"What's this?" demanded one of the searchers.

"That's a book by a Catholic theologian which explains how harmful Marxism is." Ita was clearly trembling as she answered.

"Where'd you get it?"

"My mother sent it to us." Though true, it sounded ludicrous in the situation, and Carla could not help but smile.

"What's up there?" another demanded, pointing with his gun to the closet shelf.

"Some suitcases full of clothes which belong to a friend of ours," Mary answered steadily.

"Let's have a look."

"O dear God," Carla prayed silently, "don't let them go beyond the suitcase in front." And they didn't. Strewing the contents of that one suitcase around the room seemed to satisfy them. Either they did not notice the other that held books or they had accomplished what they came to do—to terrify. Taking the book Ita's mother had sent, they started to go.

"Would you return that, please, when you've finished with it?" Ita asked. Though afraid, she tried to deal with the situation as if it were somehow normal.

Early in the morning was the best time for the military to search entire neighborhoods. The trucks and tanks would surround the area by 5:99 A.M. Then silently, in the pewter light of dawn, the soldiers would fan out. Connie thought she was dreaming one morning when she looked out her window to see camouflaged, machine-gun toting men slinking through the lanes, hugging the houses, hurrying to cover every path. Suddenly the soldiers were in position and a voice boomed over the bullhorn, "All right, all the men out into the empty lots. Hurry up! Move!"

All men, which included boys over the age of fourteen, urged along by rifle butts, were herded into a nearby soccer field. There they were lined up in alphabetical order so police records could be checked more easily. Anyone with anything recorded against him in the previous ten years was automatically taken. It did not matter if the violation was a parking ticket, robbery, or "subversive activity." Others were taken away because they resembled someone the soldiers hoped to find or looked "suspicious." All were categorized as "delinquent."

Often a search would occur on Friday—payday. Many of the men lost a week's wages for missing a day of work. They could not notify their employers; there was no phone in the neighborhood and no one was allowed to leave while the search continued.

"Go on home!" the soldiers shouted at the women and children who were anxious, unable to leave, afraid they might never see their husbands and fathers again. As the men were loaded into buses to take them to the city jail, some of the women cried out, "No! Please! He has done nothing!"

"He's a delinquent," the soldier shouted in reply.

"He's not a delinquent," a woman pleaded, "he's my son."

The next day, or several days later, some of the men were released; some were not. Those who were safe and those still waiting for news of loved ones were bonded in grief and anger and hopelessness unknown to those who have not felt the terror of repression. Ita wrote:

> Until you experience it, or somehow make someone else's experience your own, it never is truly real. The only way you and your neighbors could face up to and overcome arbitrary "fishing expeditions" and organized terror is by being very concerned for each other and by having a deep faith—not in the judicial process or human justice—but in a God who cares for his people. Of course, experiences like this among the poor and the powerless run through the Old Testament and up to today's headlines. We are privileged to have shared this, to know and feel a little of the suffering of the powerless, of those without voice.[10]

In April 1974 the bishops issued "Reconciliation in Chile," a document that called for the reestablishment of a regime with constitutional and legal guarantees for all. The document had no effect, even though a delegation of bishops met with Augusto

Pinochet and other members of the junta at the time it was issued. It seemed as if Brazilian Dom Helder Camara's prophecy that fascism would be far more threatening to the Church in Latin America than communism had indeed come true in Chile.

Church-State tensions increased even more in September 1975, when the bishops issued their most comprehensive doctrinal statement attempting to analyze the junta's ideology. "Gospel and Peace" stressed respect for the rights of human beings as an indispensable precondition for attaining peace. The right to physical and moral integrity, they continued, precludes "physical torture and terror," both of which were rampant in Chile.[11]

By the end of the year, the ecumenical Committee for Peace had been dissolved by military decree, though the work did continue as the Catholic Church assumed forms of public opposition when no other body could. Constituted by necessity as the gathering place of dissent, the mouthpiece for complaints and prophetic denunciations, and the chief conduit for the flood of money arriving from the international solidarity movements, the Church found itself in a position of enormously increased power and influence. The ecumenical Committee for Peace had been transformed into the Vicariate of Solidarity and was acclaimed internationally when awarded the United Nations Human Rights Prize in November 1978.

In the five years after the coup, repression did not lessen; it became institutionalized, and fear became part of the Chilean people. In such an atmosphere it was difficult at times for the Sisters to see many signs of hope or expect anything other than another crisis. Talking to people was no longer always therapeutic for Carla. In fact she good-naturedly sent Mary Ellen Manz a note telling her she had taken up gardening.

Occasionally they would escape for a day or weekend of relaxation and prayer. Often they went no farther than the Maryknoll Center House in Santiago to spend the day with the Sisters. There, around Easter 1975, they met Sheila Cassidy, a young British doctor who was working in a clinic in the city. Years later, Sheila sent Ita's mother a tape telling her how she had been attracted immediately to them and had accepted their invitation to visit their house in La Bandera though it was far and she was very timid about venturing beyond her daily beaten track. For the next several months, Sheila would go each week to spend an afternoon talking of all manner of things—of life and love, particularly about God and prayer and Chile. I think I spoke a lot about my own feelings of being called to religious life and they were able to laugh with me a great deal about my phobia concerning veils and long habits. At the end of the afternoon I began to feel that these were really human beings with whom I could identify. It was certainly Ita and Carla who made me feel that perhaps I could be a nun. And indeed it would perhaps be a very good thing to be.[12]

Whenever they met in La Bandera or at Sheila's, they would pray. More than once Ita chose the story of the potter in the Book of Jeremiah. It was a favorite of hers because she knew her life to be clay in the potter's hand and often preferred that it were otherwise. Ita was constantly fighting with her God who was in control of things, as absurd as they were, and wished God were less secretive about the future. "Why won't God let me read the script?" She would clench her teeth each time another unexpected event altered her life.

Carla was just the opposite. Volatile in her relationships with people and life in general, she was peacefully at home with God. When she prayed, one sensed she was where she belonged.

On October 29, 1975, Sheila was picked up by the secret police, stripped, tortured, and interrogated for having treated the bullet wound of a leader of the "opposition."

For a number of frantic days, no one knew where she was or if she were alive. Owing to a surge of international pressure, she was found, however, and when she had recovered was allowed visitors. The bleak buildings of Tres Alamos Detention Camp on the outskirts of Santiago housed more than 600 prisoners who were held without charge in accordance with the law of the state of siege. A high wall topped with barbed wire and sentry lookouts was forgotten while Ita and Carla talked with Sheila about her ordeal and that of the others they knew who had fled or "disappeared." Before they left they would unwrap, one by one, the things they had brought: chocolate, poetry books, a breviary, colored pencils, sewing materials, all of which had been roughly inspected by the guards. What they hadn't seen were the consecrated hosts that were carefully concealed in the folds of a handkerchief.

When Ita's family came to visit shortly after Sheila was released and sent home to England, Carla felt a poignant longing to see her own family again, and in the midst of that longing had a strange and disruptive experience. She was on a bus one afternoon, returning from the city to La Bandera, thinking a thousand thoughts, when all of a sudden she was overcome by an understanding of what her mother must have suffered with the birth of a daughter late in life and the death of her husband a few years later. She broke into sobs as if she were alone with no end to her tears. Weeping uncontrollably, she stumbled from the bus and hurried through the dusty streets, unashamed and finally free of the anguish over the distance between herself and her mother.

She wanted to surprise her mother and turned up at home without letting anyone know of her plans for the long-overdue visit. But it was too late. Mrs. Piette had nightmares when Carla slept in the house and during the day didn't know who her daughter was.

Almost overwhelmed by grief such as she had never known, Carla went away for thirty days of prayer and silence to consider pioneering a new mission in a *barrio* of Caracas, Venezuela. It was an appealing thought, for the continuing repression in Chile stifled creativity and made it difficult to hope. More positively, though, Carla felt that the Chilean Church had been so purified and strengthened in the present persecution that it should be sending missioners to other countries where the local churches were less aware of their mission to and for the poor and the oppressed. Tolerating no distractions whatsoever as she made this important decision, Carla even refused to see Sheila Cassidy, who had traveled halfway across the United States to find her.

When she returned to Chile, Carla wrote to Connie, who was then in the United States. "In the end I had to say no to Venezuela because I'm too weak, needy and, I guess you'd say, problematic. Home was very hard. I returned a little less than a basket case and have been recovering slowly, learning once again what it means to be poor and dependent."[13]

In August 1977, Ita was scheduled to return to New York for Reflection Year, a year of theological studies and evaluation of one's mission experience, which was required before making final vows. In lieu of the possibility of cancelling it altogether, she asked for a year's postponement. One precious year of study and reflection, she felt strongly, was too ill-proportioned a luxury in a world where many people cannot escape terror, hunger, or helplessness even for a moment. Besides, she considered that year prior to final vows to be "a very long time to reflect about something I am already convinced of."[14] But perhaps the strongest factor in her resistance was the fear that without her, Carla's heaviness and volatility might drag herself and others down. That year of grace passed quickly and, in 1978, it was Carla, as usual, who gave Ita the push she needed.

"Look, Ita," Carla told her, "you simply have to go. Don't worry about me. I'll do my best to stay out of trouble. This is something you have to do. Now go and get it over with."[15]

On her reluctant way to New York, Ita stopped in Bolivia, Peru, Nicaragua, Guatemala, and Mexico to visit friends and "to get a glimpse of what the Sisters were doing in different areas."[16]

While in Bolivia she learned more about the "Banzer Plan," the insidious design drafted by the government of Hugo Banzer Suarez with the help of the CIA. Its aim was to defame and divide the Church and in a few short years it had become operative throughout Latin America and evidently beyond. Among the fifteen points outlined in the plan are those advising that only that part of the Church which is the most progressive should be attacked.

> Attack above all the foreign clergy. Insist continuously that they are preaching armed warfare, that they are connected with international communism and have been sent to this country with the exclusive goal of moving the church toward communism . . . The CIA has decided to intervene directly in this affair. It has promised to give us information about certain priests (personal documents, studies, friends, addresses, publications, foreign contacts.) . . . Arrests should be made in the countryside, on deserted streets or late at night. Once a priest has been arrested, the Minister should plant subversive material in his briefcase and, if possible, in his room or home, and a weapon, preferably a high caliber pistol. Have a story prepared disgracing him before his bishop and the public. . . . Maintain a friendly relationship with some bishops, with certain members of the church, and with some native priests. In such a way we will assure that public opinion does not believe that there is a systematic persecution of the church but only a few of its dissident members . . . Reward the agents who best work at enforcing this plan of action by

giving them the belongings confiscated from the homes of priests and religious . . . [17]

It seemed clear to Ita that the Banzer Plan was certainly being used in Chile. When she stopped in Nicaragua to see her old friend Julie Miller, who had been assigned there from Japan several years before, she saw evidence of it there as well. Ita listened as Julie told the story of how she and another Sister had been "detained" by the National Guard when the two women tried to prevent them from taking the parish priest.

In many respects Nicaragua looked much like Chile to Ita: the ever-present military, tangible fear, cancerous suspicion, wanton disappearances. But the one big difference, the one that placed them worlds apart, was that while the Chileans had been almost hopelessly intimidated into submission by the repression, the people of Nicaragua were, as one body, heart, and voice, loudly crying out against their nearly fifty years of brutal oppression at the hands of the Somoza family. There was hope for a change in Nicaragua; that was the difference. An entire nation, with eyes on the resurrection, seemed heading toward Jerusalem.

When Ita arrived in New York, she was tired and "like a seething volcano," remembered Sister Rachel Lauze, with whom Ita studied that year.

> She was angry. The world had people in it who were beating up the poor she loved; the world had millions of other people who were closing their eyes and stopping their ears to keep from being aware of the slaughter going on. We saw a newsreel about Chile and Allende and the coup that September. At the end of it the person showing the film asked with an eager grin, "Well, how did you like it?" He thought he would spark a terrific discussion. Ita was so angry at him I thought she was going to get up and punch him in the mouth. The movie had really cut her to the heart.[18]

Ita's mother vividly remembered her daughter's state when she returned from Chile.

> We all went to meet her at the airport and I had lots of food that she especially liked. We all talked and ate but Ita didn't

talk all that much and ate only bread. I'm sure the variety and
quantity seemed extravagant. For some weeks she was depressed and we all were questioned as to why we discarded
bottles and wasted food.[19]

Ita did not know how drained she was, nor did she recognize the
full intensity of the pressures she had been under in Chile until she
was away from them. When she began her studies at Maryknoll
School of Theology, she was numb, empty, almost ready to give up,
and unable to pray. She went to the rector, Father John Patrick
Meehan, and asked for spiritual direction. Father Meehan remembered,

From the first she was very open and honest about herself and
where she was. She found prayer cold, empty, dark and
useless but kept trying. In what proved to be a short time the
Spirit began to touch her in many evident ways . . . she was
suddenly flooded with the kind of joy and love that can only
be a gift. From that point on she began to experience true
contemplative prayer and the peace, love and joy that accompany it.[20]

Though miles away from Chile and Nicaragua, Ita was vitally
concerned with the less-than-peaceful lives of her friends there.
When two of the Sisters joined a Church-sponsored hunger strike
in Santiago, Ita wrote of how hard it was to be so far away.

My only urge is to get on a plane and be with you all. There
is next to nothing in the newspapers here. One day at Mass
here the words of the consecration went booming through
me—"this is my body given for you"—the connection was
instantaneous—all those giving their bodies.[21]

As the war in Nicaragua escalated in the fall of 1978, it was very
much in the news and of personal concern to Ita and the Sisters who
had friends there. The Central American delegates to the
Maryknoll Sisters General Assembly brought firsthand reports, as
did those who returned for rest or meetings.
Sisters in the U.S. with any mission experience in Central
America were constantly called upon to give talks or workshops.

One of them, Sister Maura Clarke, with seventeen years experience in Nicaragua, would certainly never have left there had she known of the struggle her friends would take upon themselves.

"Please just say the word," she wrote to the Sisters in Nicaragua, "and I will come immediately if there is anything I can do. Oh, how difficult it is to be here at this time."

"No, Maura," they replied, "the most important thing right now is for you to do everything you can to inform the people of the U.S. of what is truly happening here."[22]

And so it was that Maura Clarke lived the painful liberation of her beloved Nicaragua from afar.

CHAPTER 6

Maura

During those increasingly tumultuous years in Nicaragua before Maura Clarke returned to the United States in October 1976, she gradually grew in her understanding of the people's struggle for freedom. "I too," she came to realize and was proud to say, "was born of gentle parents, revolutionary and poor."[1]

Tall, handsome, charming John Clarke "met his Waterloo" (as he laughingly put it)—Mary McCloskey—in 1924, during the Time of the Troubles in Ireland. After his friend was wounded during a skirmish with government troops, John carried him to a convalescent hospital in Dublin and an R.N., Mary McCloskey, let them in the back door.

Thus began a friendship that would lead to America and three children and would continue over the next 60 years.

After several years of courtship, John emigrated to New York City and was there on the dock when Mary later arrived. Mary recalled landing in lower Manhattan. The customs official, in those paternalistic days, didn't want to release a single woman into the custody of a man who was not her husband or relative. But Mary McCloskey, as a registered nurse—rare in 1928 when few women attended college—already had work, and the officials allowed her into the country.

In later years, telling the story to her grandchildren, Mary Clarke remembered that her trunks were stamped with her own initials "M.McC" because "she didn't know what would happen" when she landed in America, regardless of *who* met her on the dock.

In her eighties, Mary told this story with a smile, often when John was in the room with her.

Fortunately for John, Mary McCloskey agreed to marry him within a year and when their first child was born on January 13, 1931, it seemed as if nothing in their lives would ever matter quite so much as she. Christened Mary Elizabeth, their beautiful brown-eyed, auburn-haired daughter would thereafter always be known as Maura.

They moved to Rockaway, Queens, where often on a Sunday afternoon their friends from Ireland would visit Mary and John and their children, Maura, James, born in 1933 (known as "Buddy") and baby Julia, born in 1935 and called "Judy" by her adoring older sister.

Mary and John were gracious hosts. Whatever the hour, Mary would slip effortlessly in and out of the kitchen—and the riotous conversation—as she served sandwiches and her famous Irish soda bread.

"The thing I remember about my grandmother," says her eldest granddaughter, Patricia Keogh, "was her grace. She could oversee a dinner for twelve, teach us how to roll out pastry for an apple pie, and at the dinner table, she would joke with Grandpa and recite Yeats or Oscar Wilde."

"And she always taught us that 'family came first,' no matter what," recalls granddaughter Pamela Keogh, "that we had to stick together and help each other . . . and I think that's where Aunt Maura got some of her faith and her strength, from Grandma and Grandpa."

"We moved a number of times," John Clarke remembered years later with a laugh, "but not like the regular people. Oh, no, we moved with just a big old wagon and our friends pulling and pushing, and Rory the dog barking our way down the street, announcing our arrival for all the world to see."[2]

Maura remembered those many moves as happy times and spoke with fondness and pride of "the five Irish tinkers, so often on the move."

At Saint Francis de Sales Grade School and Stella Maris High School, Maura studied hard and did well. But she was never so intent on studies that there was not plenty of time for an outing with Father Edward Curley, or for Mission Circle, Sodality, Yearbook, and Glee Club. This last remains a bit of mystery, for though Maura loved to sing, no one remembers that she was ever able to carry a tune. But that mattered little, for her voice was certainly good enough to accompany her feet and those of her friends as they danced in the light of the street lamp long into many a summer's night.

When Maura graduated from high school, Mary Clarke remembers, "she mourned for weeks but I told her that her friends would always be her friends, and that even the girls who had entered to be nuns she could visit on a Sunday afternoon. After a while she was smiling again and went off to study to be a teacher at Saint Joseph College for Women."[3]

Midway into her freshman year, Maura was startled by her friend Maureen's question. "When are you going in?"

"In where?" Maura replied too casually.

"Into the convent."

"How did you find out?" she whispered. "My mother is the only one I've told."

"Oh, I don't know," replied Maureen, who had known her all her life. "I could just tell."

On her application to Maryknoll, Maura explained her desire with characteristic simplicity. "I want to become closer to God. I want to serve Him."[4]

And when asked why she chose a missionary community, she did not try to explain what she would never fully understand. "I am attracted to it," was her clear-cut reply, "and I feel I could do this type of work."[5]

When asked why she had not finished school before applying, Maura explained that she thought it "impractical to spend my parents' hard-earned money when I could not repay them . . . I am stopping school this term and I am going to begin working to save some money for entering if I am accepted."[6]

Maura was accepted at Maryknoll in 1950 and got a job in the billing department at Saks Fifth Avenue while waiting for her entrance date. Typically, though, she did not save a dime but bought presents for her parents and Judy and Buddy.

"It was a nice September day in 1950 and the sun was shining," Mary Clarke remembered clearly some thirty years later. "And we drove up there to Maryknoll in a few cars with several groups of friends. Maura wore a green suit and I remember telling her that day that if she couldn't last it out and become a nun, she shouldn't be discouraged. She should come right back to me and become a teacher."[7]

Maura did more than merely "last it out." In fact, Sister Maura John Clarke, as she was named on reception day, lived religious life as well as she possibly could because that was precisely what God had asked her to do, and that made her happy. Yet while she never really questioned the clarity of God's call, she tended throughout her life to underestimate the quality of her response.

"I was entirely too docile as a novice," Maura remembered many years later, "and the novitiate took away something of my confidence and personality. Among so many religious and rules I felt rather lost but I conformed."[8] She is remembered as having done everything fervently, from sprinkling the novices' curtained cells with holy water, to praying the breviary, to scouring an already (to her eye at least) immaculate sink. It was in this area of housekeeping that Sr. Maura John's obedience shone, for she was not overly domestic. One day, however, she did seriously wonder at the extremes to which a love of cleanliness and order could go, though Maura never questioned what she and her work group had been asked to do. They went, in double file and silence, to remove the oak leaves from the path that wound through the woods. It did look much nicer, she had to admit. Only later did she realize that the task had not been to clean the forest floor but to gather mulch for the rhododendrons at the front of the house. And though Maura would laugh as she told this and other stories about herself in the years to come, she never lost her gullibility. She simply believed what she was told, dealt with what was evident, and only seldom, if ever, doubted anyone or anything.

In the spring of 1954, Maura completed her studies at Maryknoll Teachers College and was looking forward to being assigned. Though she had hoped to be sent to Africa, Maura knew it was "the will of God" and was therefore not overly disappointed when assigned to teach in Saint Anthony of Padua School in the Bronx.

Officially classified as "mission territory" by the archdiocese of New York, the high-crime, low-income neighborhood of 166th Street and Prospect Avenue was one step up and midway on a major migratory route from Harlem to St. Alban Parish on Long Island. In those preliberation days of the mid-fifties, when the Reverend Martin Luther King, Jr., was virtually unknown beyond the boundaries of his Selma, Alabama, parish, the unquestioned goal of the "Negroes" and Puerto Ricans was to "make it" in a white society, a society made more accessible to them by the parish school that was staffed by the Sisters. Though a free public school was only blocks away, enrollment at St. Anthony's climbed steadily until there were 475 students by the time Maura arrived in 1955.

"She was an excellent first grade teacher," one of the Sisters recalled, "principally because she was as spontaneous as the children. Though her teaching methods were at first rather haphazard and her room apparently devoid of discipline, she was able to teach and the children able to learn. They loved her."[9]

Owing to the structure of religious life, the demands of the school, and the dangers of the neighborhood, St. Anthony's was an island for the Sisters in that volatile world, just as it was an oasis for the parishioners who participated in the Legion of Mary, Credit Union, Parent-Teacher Association, Spanish Instruction Group, Scouts, sports teams, and choir.

Beyond the red brick walls, drugs, prostitution, related crimes, and the accompanying violence—though camouflaged by day—raged undisguised at night.

The sounds of shattering glass, screeching tires, drunken cries, a shot in the night were so common that a certain insensitivity toward tragedy seemed to hang in the air. Maura never grew accustomed to hearing the children's stories about their mothers being beaten, their fathers slashed, their brothers shot, their sisters raped. At first she was incredulous and then saddened when she realized how many women had children by several men and saw how many children were apparently deprived of the love with which she had been lavished.

"Sister," a surprisingly obstinate little boy called out in class one day, "if God's a father, Sister, I don't want nothing to do with him and I sure don't want him messing around with me!" That bothered Maura so much that she consulted widely and for weeks to find a way to convince that child of God's love.[10]

The atmosphere in which many of her children lived was one Maura had never felt before and found hard to understand. Even though she clearly saw and deeply felt the suffering that people could inflict upon each other, which life often seemed to dispense at random, she lived as if evil were less real than goodness, as if tenderness were stronger than violence and joy longer-lasting than pain.

She dealt with wrongs as if they were merely mistakes. "That's all right, Franklin," she comforted a second grade embezzler. "I'm sure you won't lose the money again. Here are some more raffle books for you to sell."[11] Needs, it seemed, were something Maura considered to have been made for her to fill. Almost never did she ferret out the cause of a need or suspect the legitimacy of a request for help. She received every person who knocked at the door as if she had invited them to come and had been waiting.

"Sister is the most selfless, generous, outgoing person I have ever known" reads an evaluation done prior to Maura's final vows. "Her only fault, from my observation, is that she never thinks of keeping her own self together and sometimes goes off in something not quite recognizable as a Maryknoll habit. Just the same, she is an easy person to be with and a very fine Sister. I highly recommend her for final profession."[12]

These evaluations were written in 1959, five years after Maura had begun teaching at Saint Anthony's. Each year, as the time for assignments drew close, Maura waited to see if her name would be on the list. "It was something you longed for," Maura remembered many years later. "All of us wanted to go to an overseas mission. Every year we were waiting for assignment."[13] In the spring of 1959 the word arrived: "Sister Maura John Clarke, assigned to teach in Maryknoll School, Siuna, Nicaragua."

It was harder than she anticipated to say good-bye to her parents, but they were proud of their daughter and that gave her the courage to go. The good-byes were softened, too, by the company of Sister Maura Kathleen Kelly from Chicago, whom Maura had recently met and with whom she would be close friends for the rest of her life.

Though Maura and "Kay," as Sister Maura Kathleen would be called, found it necessary to consult a map in order to find Nicaragua and wondered why Siuna had not been given a dot, they nonetheless had heard of that little jungle mining town, known to be one of the poorest and most isolated of the Maryknoll Sisters' missions.

CHAPTER 7

Siuna

In 1944, Sister Marie Estelle Coupe headed a community of Sisters assigned to Nicaragua to staff the first parochial school in that country. Though the Sisters were the first North American women religious to work there, other North Americans—the United States Marines—had been in Nicaragua since 1912 in order to keep that strategically and economically important country in accord with the interests of the United States. When the chief patriot, anti-imperialist Augusto Cesar Sandino, was murdered in 1934, the Marines trained a National Guard as their replacement, put the North American-educated Anastasio Somoza Garcia, a former toilet inspector and one-time currency counterfeiter, in charge, and withdrew. In 1937 Somoza consolidated his power by having himself elected president and by 1944, when the Maryknoll Sisters arrived, was already forging what was to become the longest dynastic dictatorship in Latin America.

When the Sisters reached Managua they were disappointed to learn that due to wartime shortages, the convent in Siuna would not be ready for some months. Nonetheless, they enjoyed the delay by becoming acquainted with the language, the capital city and surrounding countryside, and the Assumption Sisters, who would be their good friends for many years. They also had occasion to meet President and Mrs. Somoza.

"A major event in the lives of the Maryknoll Sisters in Nicaragua," reads the diary for December 17, 1944, "a visit to the Presidential Palace. . . ."[1]

Arriving in the president's car, the Sisters were greeted by Mrs. Somoza, "La Presidenta," and escorted past the guards to the reception room where they awaited the arrival of the president, "a dignified figure in his military garb," the diary continues. "He is a very amiable person, educated in the States and speaking fine English."

During lunch he entertained the Sisters with an account of his trip to the United States following his inauguration and told of the great acclaim paid him in Washington. Turning then to the Sisters' work, President Somoza spoke highly of the tremendous progress the Church was making in the little pueblo of Siuna and throughout the vicariate of Bluefields on the Atlantic Coast. "I would like to visit there some day," he told the Sisters, "but meanwhile if there is anything at all which I can do to help your community in that admirable work, please do not hesitate to approach me."

"We are not looking for special privileges," Sister Marie Estelle assured him, "nor do we contemplate reform. We have come simply to help your people in whatever way we can."

"That is very sweet of you to say." He was charming and charmed.

Later in the week, the Sisters were again picked up at the convent by the president's private limousine and escorted by an armored car to Montelima, his country home, where they enjoyed a "simple meal" with the Somozas and United States Ambassador Mr. Stewart. During the meal La Presidenta proudly passed around a Christmas card that had just arrived from their son, who was studying at West Point. Then the president invited the Sisters to his garden, where he proudly showed them the giant sunflowers. "These do not always grow well here, but mine are thriving and bigger than anyone can believe. Here, I will give you some seeds which I want you to plant in your garden in Siuna," he said as he poured them into Sister Marie Estelle's hand. "We will compete to see who can produce the heartier and more enduring plant."

On Christmas Eve, 1944, the six Sisters boarded a small one-engine plane and, with their dreams and seeds, were on their way to Siuna. "The trip, scarcely two hours, seemed at times interminable," continues the diary. As the plane dipped and droned above the mountains and the dense jungle, the Sisters held on and pointed when there was something other than the forest to see—a tiny clearing, a house, a wisp of smoke.

"Over there," the pilot shouted through the motor's din, "that's Siuna." Circling the town they saw La Luz, the gold mining area surrounded by shacks, and up above it "the Zone" where Canadian mine officials and their families lived in another world. Then they saw the little pueblo of Siuna "sadly settled in its little hole" and over against the mountain the new convent that the people of Siuna had built for the Sisters. As they approached the dusty landing strip they saw "little dots hurrying along the road." The people of La Luz and Siuna were coming to meet the plane.

On closer inspection, the world in which these people lived was as drab a place as could be found anywhere. Ill-paid miners lived in rows of unpainted, rat-infested company houses. Mosquitoes thrived. Parasitic infections were rampant due to lack of sanitation. Bars and *cantinas* provided the only recreation. There was no transportation to other towns except by costly airplane travel. Morals were at a low ebb. Mortality rates were high. None of the children and few of the parents had any education whatsoever. The original settlers, having been drawn from the unemployed in scattered places, had no common heritage except privation. There was a complete cultural lag. A sociologist assigned to study the area had pronounced Siuna to be "sociologically hopeless."[2]

Fifteen years later, however, when Maura Clarke arrived and Sister Marie Estelle had gone to pioneer a new mission in Chile, some things had changed in Siuna. There was a clinic that cared for an average of a thousand people a month, or roughly one-fifth of the total population of that undernourished, disease-infested settlement. School was a source of pride and hope for those parents who had no education and saw it as a bridge over which their children would cross from the lifelong misery they had known to a brighter future. Though Maura's young and illiterate students were far more fluent in Spanish than she, communication was not a problem. Maura wrote to her parents:

One dear little farm boy, Natividad, came the other day for his religion class. He stood there all ragged but happily smiling with his gift of a little bag of bread that he had bought in the pueblo for the Madres. Today he came with big tears to ask for a coffin and clothes for his baby brother who had died this morning. When I told him that he now has a little saint in heaven, he answered, "I have four."

While a group of little boys was practicing for the reception of their First Holy Communion, Sister Jude Christine and I encountered a big coral snake coiled up close to the altar. Sister hurled a rock while I dropped one from above. The one

hundred little fellows sitting in the church benches clapped
at the performance, but on the walk home, Jose, age 8, who
has already killed several snakes, said, "You know that snake
you killed, Madre? It was already dead."[3]

Though the children would always be Maura's most refreshing
source of joy, she delighted in everyone she met and easily formed
friendships that lasted for years. One of her friends was the wife of
the Canadian director of the mine. She gave generously of her time
in helping Sister Rita Owczarek, from Chicago, in the clinic, and
offered the use of one of the houses in "the Zone" whenever the
Sisters might want to get away for a day of meetings or prayer. They
took advantage of that offer once or twice but felt awkward there
and preferred not to go. When invited to a mine official's home for
dinner, Maura and her Sisters were startled and ashamed to find
themselves being served an elaborate meal of filet mignon by one
of their undernourished neighbors from "down below."

"The Zone," with its golf course, private club, manicured lawns,
and plush homes transplanted from suburban Canada, was con-
spicuously and cruelly out of context in Siuna. No one could pass
the National Guard sentry except the Canadian families, their
guests, and the "Siunites" who worked there as maids, cooks,
gardeners, and baby-sitters. As one mine official once explained,
"You are down here for charity, Sister; we are here for business."

Over the years, John and Mary Clarke visited Siuna twice,
staying in the convent once and in an empty house in "the Zone"
the second time. Mary remembered:

Siuna was simply another world. People living behind boards.
There must have been one hundred people out to meet the
plane. Those people with large, lovely bright eyes and bellies
swollen from malnutrition. And always so polite. Starving and
polite. The house we stayed in the second time had everything. It was beside a pool and had a General Electric refrig-
erator and stove. Everything we didn't have at home we had
there.[4]

It was generally known that the company divided the profits
from the gold mine with the increasingly powerful Somoza family

while the miners received pathetic wages and were paid only until such time as they almost inevitably contracted a lung disease.

There had been attempts to form unions at La Luz Mines in the mid-1950s, but Somoza's National Guard had taken care of the troublemakers and things had been quiet ever since. Meanwhile, for the Sisters and priests, there were the sick to care for, people in need of the sacraments and religious instruction, and the children to educate so they could look forward to working above ground. Some miners' children were already employed in secretarial positions with the company. Others felt they had enough schooling to escape to the busier parts of Nicaragua to look for work. A few were in Bluefields or Managua continuing their education. Others returned to teach in Siuna.

With the comings and goings in the little pueblo, ugly rumors drifted back from the cities, and stories were told of tortures, killings, "disappearances" at the hands of the National Guard. When General Anastasio Somoza Garcia was killed in 1956 by a lone idealistic poet, his two sons, Luis and Anastasio Somoza Debayle, had three thousand "suspects" arrested and tortured in a brutal attempt to protect the family fortune and power. Among them were unsympathetic merchants and professional people who might pose a threat.

Other stories of occasional unrest came only faintly and from far away to the American Sisters isolated in Siuna, but they seemed too insubstantial and too terrible to believe. Besides, the Sisters knew the president, Anastasio Somoza Debayle, who had succeeded his father and brother. It had been a big day when he visited Siuna. And though most of his time was spent in "the Zone," he had stopped at the school and had certainly shown himself to be as charming as his father.

Members of the ill-famed National Guard were known to the Sisters too. In fact the local *comandante* was so distraught by the death of President Kennedy in 1963 that he had gone to speak with the Sisters at the convent. He and all the local National Guard were in the church with everyone in town for a memorial mass in honor of President Kennedy, and the Sisters were proud to see the Nicaraguan and American flags waving side by side and to hear both anthems played. Somoza had even sent troops to assist the Americans in the Bay of Pigs, and the American Capuchin pastor of Siuna, a chaplain in the Nicaraguan Army, had gone along as well. To the

Sisters, derogatory tales about Somoza seemed beyond belief in the face of what they knew from firsthand experience.

Besides, as religious, the Sisters were not to be concerned with politics, but only with forming the laity in the faith so they could assume their proper Christian role in society. That is precisely what Maura was doing with the children in the school until a telegram arrived from Maryknoll, N.Y., in 1962: "Sister Maura John Clarke is assigned to be principal of the school and superior of the community in Siuna, Nicaragua."

"There simply must be some mistake." Incredulous, Maura stared at the telegram. She did not want to believe news that would limit her time with the children in the classroom and change her relationship with her Sisters and friends. Besides, she knew that any one of the other Sisters, most of whom were older and more experienced in mission than she, would have been a better superior. That belief rested not so much on a low self-image as on her sincere respect and appreciation for everyone else. Every bit of humble, appreciative Maura was uncomfortable with being "superior" to her Sisters, and that proved to be the secret of her success. "I'll accept this as the will of God," Maura relented when she finally believed it was true, "but each of you has to help me."[5]

One of the persistent and burning issues of those years had to do with the Sisters' life-style and their closer identification with the people whom they had come to serve. Some felt that it was only prudent to continue to live in a house with a stove and running water and plumbing, to continue to receive canned goods from the United States and Managua, and to be able to escape to the city for a rest or medical attention. Others felt that the house, the food, the freedom of movement all served to distance them from the people with whom they had come to share life as closely as possible. Perhaps the most serious charge was that the Sisters' relative abundance established and maintained a relationship with the people that more closely resembled that of benefactor to charity case than of friend to friend. Such a relationship was both oppressive and demeaning. Maura heard what some of the Sisters clearly saw, and yet she could never refrain from "giving a handout" to whoever asked for anything.

She had always been a "pushover" for anyone truly in need or merely smart enough to take advantage of a soft and gullible heart. After giving away her toothpaste, hairbrush, and the last of her monthly allowance, Maura would borrow whatever she needed from her Sisters or ask for an advance on next month's allowance, gradually losing track of what month she had last advanced upon. Sometimes impatient with Maura's galloping generosity, the Sisters would again point out to her that it might be best to address the causes of the people's needs instead of prolonging dependencies.

But whatever the discussion—life-style, authority, mission among the poor, religious life—Maura was part of the search and, as superior, would encourage all to express their ideas, "There are many things not quite the way they should be, too many people suffering, and yet the answers are not clear. We will just have to keep asking and searching, knowing that God forgives our mistakes."[6]

Maura's many letters during these years are, typically, expressions of affection and appreciation for the recipient of the letter and full of inquiries about the health of Irish relatives, the activities of nieces and nephews, and the well-being of her parents. Only seldom does a letter convey any adequate information about life in Siuna and the events that filled her day. And almost never does she indicate what those events might mean to her. One such letter— remarkable for the number of important topics she touched upon all at once—was written to her sister, Judy Clarke Keogh, in 1967. In it she spoke of the pain of the growth in religious life, the awakening of the *pueblo*, and the beginnings of new works outside of the school and clinic.

> As you have been reading in all the magazines, etc., there is much tension and change in religious life. This of course is affecting Maryknoll and all of us, but is for our good because in all growth or change there has to be pain. Religious communities and the many other structures in the Church need renewal and perhaps a revolution in order to give them new life and help us all to be Christians meeting the needs of today.
>
> My goodness, this sounds strange, I suppose, but it is uppermost in our thoughts so you'll understand.
>
> We have just three years of high school (but already) the people in the pueblo are beginning to unite and to make their

voices heard. Siuna has been abandoned for so long but there is an awakening of hope.

Two of our Sisters have been released from schoolwork and are constantly out on mission trips—horseback, river boat, etc.[7]

In a vicariate such as Bluefields, where the kind and aging bishop considered nothing more vital or urgent than teaching in the parochial school, "release from schoolwork for mission trips" was bound to become an issue. It was such an issue, and apparently so impossible to resolve, that several Sisters eventually asked to be assigned elsewhere. For over a year the differences brewed and bothered all concerned, yet the priests and Sisters who were in Siuna at the time remember that it was Maura who seemed to suffer most, who felt conflict most acutely. Her inability to be less than forthright and honest was in constant tension with her fear of hurting anyone.

During the summer of 1968 Maura wrote to her parents of the difficulties and expressed a conviction from which no amount of suffering could cause her to waver.

Keep Siuna especially in your prayers as we are thinking seriously that it might be best to leave as a community for the good of the Church. Missioners are supposed to work themselves out of a job. The school is being completely handled by lay teachers. Pray that God's will be done. It is so hard to go. [8]

The going became all the more difficult in the wake of what occurred on August 11, 1968. Maura wrote to her parents on August 25:

We had some terribly violent rainstorms almost two weeks ago, breaking the dam in El Salto which provides all the electric power for the mine here in Siuna. The rush of the flooding dam and river completely wiped out several little *pueblos,* all of the houses of the people and their belongings … All our bridges were washed away and all communication cut off … All these poor people have lost everything but their lives. They were taken in by families here in the *pueblo* and are receiving some food and clothing, but what of the future?[9]

It was simply not profitable for the company to repair the mine. For the people of Siuna and La Luz—every one of whom was directly or indirectly dependent upon the mine for a livelihood—the future loomed dismal indeed. In a desperate attempt to do the impossible, twelve men went to Managua to beg help from Somoza's government. "Pray that we can awaken the government to help their own people in a more stable way," Maura naively wrote to her parents. "It seems as though the will of God is that Maryknoll leave Siuna. The word finally came and the bishop agrees that it would probably be best if we leave after the school closes in December. It seems very sad to leave now after what has happened."[10] And yet, the Sisters recognized that something creative was occurring as well.

Julio Charrarria, a simple man, a miner all his adult life, was easy to overlook. He stood up in a town assembly one night and said, "I have worked eighteen years for the Company, but what do I have? Nothing! Let the company go. Let's stand on our own two feet."[11]

Hearing that determination in the voice of the *pueblo*, the Sisters were less reluctant to leave.

> Perhaps by our very presence we have unconsciously assumed leadership which might well have been taken over by the people. If that is so, our withdrawal may bring forth the seed which was planted and has been lying dormant for the twenty-four years in which we have worked in this mission.[12]

"Final departure was on December 16, 1968," the closing lines of the Siuna diary read. "Many of our Siuna friends, teachers, parents, and children were at the airfield to wave good-bye, thus closing this beautiful chapter of Maryknoll history of twenty-four years of loving service in Siuna."[13]

After closing the Maryknoll Sisters' mission, Maura returned to Maryknoll, New York, to report on the final events, make her annual retreat, and visit with her family. She was with her parents when her mother became quite ill, and so Maura asked permission to remain a while longer in order to care for her. By the end of 1969, when Mary was much improved and Maura anxious to return to

Nicaragua, it took nothing more than a short note from her good friend Sister Jude Christine ("Bea") Zaragoza, originally from San Francisco, to trigger Maura's decision. "We are beginning a new work in Miralagos," Bea wrote, "a poor *barrio* on the edge of Lake Managua, and we would love for you to join us."[14]

CHAPTER 8

Earthquake

When Maura returned to Nicaragua, she was not the same woman who arrived there eleven years before. "She had been greatly influenced by the poverty in Nicaragua," Maura's sister, Judy, remembered, "and had come to see that unless the overall situation was changed, the missioners just kept doing the same things over and over again without really making any difference at all."[1]

The poverty and oppression to which Maura returned was much the same as she had known in Siuna, perhaps even worse in the cities where contrasts were blatant and the causes less difficult to identify.

The economic "progress" of the 1950s and 1960s poured wealth into the lives of a few while a steadily growing percentage of the population slipped more deeply into misery. Thousands of people expelled from their lands by Somoza's agro-industrial projects squatted where they could while looking for work. Some of those people were living in the parish of Santo Domingo in the *barrio* of Miralagos when Maura arrived to join Sisters Bea Zaragoza and Rita Owczarek in February 1970.

Ten years in Siuna had not accustomed Maura to the misery in which the people there were forced to live. She wrote to her parents in the spring of 1970:

> The area where we live is filled with poor people living in tents and shacks and just waiting for the government to give them the land they promised. Some live in one-room hovels, very dark and miserable. Many of the little children run around dirty and naked while their mothers try to sell some fruit or baked goods in the market. I am trying to get to know them and after a while we hope to begin having meetings with

them to form the "Family of God" which is a way of trying to unite them to solve their own problems and to be formed in their faith through discussions at night.[2]

Though Maura was happy that the families were gradually being moved from their "tents and the worst huts" to a tract of dry land outside the city, she was at the same time sad to see them go.

There were other movements underway as well. In October 1970, a group of students and several priests who were tired of the repression took over a number of churches in the city of Managua.

"Actually there really weren't any riots when they took over the churches and the cathedral in protest to violations of human rights," Maura wrote to her parents.

> It was a very peaceful and disciplined protest and showed that the Church, represented by the six priests who stayed with the students, was committed to the poor and the suffering, in contrast to the former image of a Church tied to the apron strings of a corrupt government. Don't worry. I'll be careful and stay out of the riots and fights but we must do what we can to lend support to those who have the courage to give themselves for a change, as surely this can't continue . . . A sad thing happened shortly after the incident of the churches. Four of our bishops, who are quite conservative, denounced the action of the priests and students and thus showed themselves as siding with the government against most of the people of God who stood with the protestors. It was too bad they just didn't keep silent.[3]

Shortly thereafter, Maura was invited to attend the National Youth Congress for young men and women from all parts of Nicaragua. "It was an inspiring experience and a great success," Maura wrote.

> The young people of Nicaragua are very conscious of the injustice of their government and the related misery of the poor, and they are willing to give their lives for change. They are very desirous at the same time of doing it completely as Christ offered himself.[4]

By the end of October the rainy season had filled the lake to overflowing and the still-inhabited homes were filled with polluted water. Eventually, the Sisters and three hundred of their neighbors from the shantytown were relocated on the site of a former cotton plantation twelve kilometers outside the city.

The "Operacion Permanente de Emergencia Nacional" (Permanent Operation of National Emergency), popularly called "OPEN," was a vast checkerboard of 2,400 lots, each 30 by 10 meters. Once these were filled, OPEN was expanded to miles of dusty little wooden shacks. "It is a rapidly growing town of our poorest market people," Maura wrote. "There is no light or water in the settlement but there is a great spirit of hopefulness among the people as the little plot of land will one day be their own."[5]

Everything in the Sisters' plywood house was covered with sheets of plastic, a pretense of protection from the dust that seeped constantly and sometimes billowed in. Each bed was covered with the same dusty plastic, which was removed very gingerly at night so as to disturb the dust as little as possible.

Maura seemed not to notice the discomfort of the house and wrote only, "You'd get a kick out of this funny little house."[6]

She enjoyed living in OPEN and loved the people who continued to move in each day. Yet the three-hour round-trip to her work in Miralagos was increasingly impractical as political turmoil and transportation strikes caused the buses to be less and less predictable.

When Kay Kelly, her friend from Siuna days, was returning to Nicaragua from the United States, she and Maura made plans to move into a house closer to their work in the parish of Santo Domingo. Sister Melba Bantay, originally from Manila, Philippines, also joined them.

For a year Maura, Kay, and Melba were busy with adult groups in the barrio and delighted with their house, which was accessible and open to their neighbors. It was with reluctance that they decided to move to the third floor of the new parish center in Managua, an offer they could not in conscience turn down, since the apartment was free and the money they would otherwise pay for rent could be used for parish projects among the poor. "I wish you could see our new penthouse apartment," Maura wrote to her sister, betraying not a hint of disappointment. "It is simple but nicely painted and very roomy so that when the Sisters come into the city there will be plenty of room for them."[7]

On the evening of December 22, 1972, Melba, Maura, and Kay had finished their supper and prayed and were talking of the day's activities. Kay was fidgety and distracted, not at all like herself.

"What's the matter, Kay?" Maura asked, concerned.

"I don't know what it is. I'm jumpy for some reason. Maybe I'll just take an aspirin and go to bed early. Sleep well. I'll see you in the morning."[8]

The slight tremor they had felt earlier in the evening was not uncommon, and they had forgotten about it by the time they went to bed. The radio stations were advising the residents of Managua not to lock their doors in case they had to flee during the night. But the Sisters had not listened to the news.

At 12:28 the earthquake struck. "Get up!" Kay yelled the others awake. "We have to get out of here!"

They heard the low rumbling of the earth, the sound of the city falling and the people crying out in fear and pain. And they felt that terrible sensation that there is nothing firm in the world. Running as best they could down the swaying, shifting stairs, they reached the first floor only to realize that no one had a key to unlock the front door. They were trapped. By then the violent shaking had subsided and Melba braved the climb back up and returned with the key which no longer fit in the damaged door.

Maura wrote to her parents on Christmas, three days later.

I thought that was our end. We were frightened when with all of the efforts of the priests we couldn't get out of any door of the house. Another tremor came and we feared the house would crush us. Finally, we climbed out the window of the second floor after breaking the glass. We had to tie sheets together to slide down and with the help of the priests and a small ladder we got down to the ground. Our whole city came down in a few seconds. Many, many people were crushed to death. Everyone ran all over trying to rescue people from below the cement walls crushing them. One of the young men of the community was crushed under a giant concrete wall and I thought he could never be saved.[9]

As the men tried the impossible task of lifting the cement wall from Sergio's back, Maura held his hand and prayed with him, apparently unconcerned that another tremor might crush them all. "I witnessed a miracle," Maura continued, "when a few of the men with old crude jacks and the strength of Samson inched the wall off Sergio a tiny bit so he could breathe and then finally he crawled out with only a broken arm and leg."[10]

Melba, Maura, and Kay moved back to the Sisters' house in OPEN, "the poor despised barrio" that became the haven for the displaced from the city. By day the Sisters did what they could to provide shelter, food, and medical treatment for OPEN's new residents. It was difficult to help, however, because the government did not want the Sisters or priests involved with the distribution of the food and clothing arriving from all over the world.

Following the destruction of much of the capital city, Somoza had declared martial law, enforced strict censorship of the press, and suspended all constitutional rights—all of which unequivocally proclaimed that he had so little popular support he had to turn to repression to stay in power. Whatever popular support he did have before the earthquake quickly dissipated as virtually nothing was done to respond to the critical needs of the people. Somoza made himself solely responsible for the millions of dollars in international aid that came pouring into the country and conveniently syphoned off most of it for himself and the National Guard. But perhaps his crucial error was to establish his own bank, insurance company, and finance and construction firms, thereby growing rich while isolating himself from the business people of Nicaragua who had previously given him support.

The Church, too, through local personnel and international relief agencies, came into closer contact with the people's misery and identified the systematic violence of the Somoza regime as its principal cause. Church support, which had been waning since the 1968 Episcopal Conference in Medellín, Colombia, shifted to an overt challenge and critique of the Somoza regime.

Early in January 1973, at the invitation of a North American architect working with the United States Army Engineering team helping to build refugee camps, Maura, Melba, and two of the parish priests moved into Campamento Esperanza, one of the many tent camps that had been erected to accommodate the 100,000 people who were homeless and mourning 10,000 dead. When the Nicaraguan military personnel discovered Church personnel working as volunteers in the camp, they forbade them to have anything to do with the kitchen or the distribution of clothes. Nor could the Sisters and priests meet with the people in groups to find solutions to their problems, or even to pray or read the Bible; that would be considered "subversive." Even the idea of a summer school for the children was too touchy an activity to attempt. In spite of the difficulties, there was more than enough to do. The carpenters in the camp were organized to build more stable quarters, a kitchen, and latrines. Women met to make small articles to sell for an income. Children were allowed to play. The task of organizing teams to clean the camp was unending. Though no one expected to be in the camp for long, the people were distraught by the news of another move at the end of March.

"We just received word that the people have to be out of their tents and moved to another temporary housing project within twenty-four hours," Maura wrote to her brother, Bud. "This came as a terrible shock because they aren't ready to move." Even more to the point, the people did not have the money with which to pay the rent for the tiny wooden dirt-floor houses into which they were being relocated.

"The reason for the hurry in getting them out," Maura continued, "is that the American Embassy is building on the neighboring property and they don't want these people next door. This is very unjust but there is little we can do here in Nicaragua except, God willing, to help the poor to gain confidence in themselves and to unite in a peaceful but strong protest."[11]

As the people from Campamento Esperanza were transferred to their new little shacks not far from the polluted shore of Lake Managua, Maura and Melba again joined Kay and the other Sisters in OPEN. That shantytown had grown enormously in the wake of the city's destruction and was now a concentration of 25,000 poor people from all parts of Nicaragua. Maura would live and work with them for the next three years.

CHAPTER 9

Signs of Struggle

When Maura returned to OPEN in March 1973, she was immediately "back home again."

She loved working with the youth group and meeting with the Christian community in different sections of the barrio. Once in a while she would have to give a talk and for those occasions she would labor many long hours, often right up until the last minute, in order to have her thoughts well chosen, organized, and clear. She took that preparation so seriously that she would sometimes do the uncharacteristic thing of asking the Sisters to tell whoever might come for her that she was busy. "No, please don't tell them that I'm not home, just tell them that I am behind in preparing for tonight's meeting and that I would love to see them tomorrow." If callers insisted, however, Maura would receive them as if she had all the time in the world.[1]

Though solitude came less seldom than people, Maura loved and needed it just as much. Prior to the annual regional meetings, the Sisters would usually schedule two or three days of quiet and prayer. On those days, Maura would disappear with her Bible and her lunch and walk for hours along the Pacific beach. Sometimes, since Sister Marie Estelle had returned to Nicaragua, Maura would go to the new mission in Leon to enjoy the space of another's house, write letters, and read. Estelle was Maura's refuge, the one with whom she could be as others were with her, vulnerable and self-revealing. Maura, who was shy of any limelight or attention, found Estelle's scrutiny and clear advice a comfort. And Estelle, the strong woman who had been formed by her role as superior in Hawaii, Nicaragua, and Chile, could be exactly who she was with Maura. They were two very different women who were simply at home with each other.

As the situation in the country deteriorated, Maura's usually effervescent letters carried hints of moments and even days when her spirits were low. And yet she would always pull herself up, remembering what the people of Nicaragua seemed innately to believe: that victory would emerge from their suffering and struggle.

Maura wrote two years after the earthquake:

> This Christmas we have so much to give thanks for. In spite of all the problems about us: the lack of jobs, the terrible injustices against the poor, the contrast of the very few rich having so much and the millions of poor not having the security of the next meal, we feel an ever-increasing hope which only belongs to those who know that Christ is here and coming. How very privileged we are to live and work among the poor. How many lessons they give us with their spirit of simplicity and joy.[2]

As the struggle against Somoza grew in the days before Christmas, the Democratic Union of Liberation was created under the leadership of Pedro Joaquin Chamorro, editor of the opposition newspaper *La Prensa*. Conservatives, Liberal Democrats, Christian and Social Democrats, and even the Nicaraguan Socialist Party converged to form UDEL, uniting around a platform calling for the recovery of democratic rights and social and economic transformation of society.

During the same month, the "Sandinistas" made a move that rallied the country to new hope. The Sandinista Front for National Liberation, "the Frente," named for Augusto Cesar Sandino, the anti-imperialist hero who was killed by General Anastasio Somoza in 1934, initially operated as mountain-based guerrilla bands along the Nicaraguan-Honduran border. Following two years of military failures and hardships as they clashed with National Guard and Honduran Army units in 1961-1962, FSLN focused for a time on political action in the city and then returned to the mountains in 1967. Until 1974 the FSLN was "accumulating force in silence," building up organizations of students, workers, Christian and cultural groups that would be the link between the "the Frente" and the people. That silence was broken in December 1974, when the Sandinistas interrupted a Christmas party being held for the American Ambassador. *Los Muchachos* ("the boys," Sandinista freedom fighters) demanded a sum of $10 million, the release of all political prisoners, safe conduct for themselves and the political prisoners to Cuba, and broadcasting for five days over all TV and radio stations the crimes committed by the National Guard under martial law. With Archbishop Obando y Bravo mediating, all demands, short of the total sum of $10 million, were met.

On the morning of December 28, Maura turned on the radio. "Come listen to this, Kay. I don't believe it." They were incredulous, but it was true. The brutal parade of atrocities performed by Somoza's National Guard for many long years was being proclaimed across the country. The jubilation in the hearts of the Nicaraguan people over this bold challenge to Somoza was hushed by their fear of reprisals and their fear of disappointment if their hopes were crushed again. As the bus carrying "the boys" traveled through Managua en route to the airport, the silent crowds signaled "V" for Victory, their tears of joy and gratefulness flowing freely, for now they knew that something could be done. Following this FSLN victory, a state of siege was declared which, in practical terms, meant a mounting of the already familiar repression.

In June of that year and for the next several months, the story of the rape of Amada Pineda became the focus of the Sisters' energies and drew the attention of the entire country. Maura wrote to her parents in June 1974:

> There has been a great deal of turmoil over a very tragic case of a *campesina* woman of about 30 named Amada. She was taken into custody unjustly by the National Guard under suspicion of belonging to a union of farmers or something. She was raped by 15 soldiers, a few of them officers, for about three or four days. This is one case but there are so many like it. The other women are afraid to reveal such a thing. This young woman is beautiful and has a striking natural dignity. We went to court to support her.[3]

Amada told the Sisters that she was determined to go through with the trial in order to publicize at least one of the innumerable cases of rape by members of the National Guard against women, including little girls, old women, and pregnant mothers. She had nothing to lose, she said, for her life was already ruined.

The people were united in their support of Amada and grateful for her courage. Her trial, together with "the boys' " front-page exploits and Pedro Joaquin Chamorro's relentless pursuit and publication of the truth, all combined to unite the Nicaraguan people and to enlist international support for their struggle against Somoza.

The fact that every effort at change was labeled as "communist inspired" by the government only spurred more and more Christian communities into deeper and more active commitment to the poor in urban neighborhoods. "Delegates of the Word," or lay ministers, were intensifying their efforts at social improvements among the plantation workers and *campesinos.*

The Christian community of OPEN impressed upon Maura what the Sisters had been trying to tell her for years: giving material goods is not always the most effective means of dealing with want. "You are always ready to give us bread and shoes and money," some young men in the Christian community said to her one day, "but maybe it would be better for all of us to try to understand why it is that we are poor and to look for solutions together."[4]

In the summer of 1976 both the effectiveness and the difficulties of united neighborhood efforts became clear in OPEN as the barrio rallied around the "water fight." When the water company of Managua tried to charge the residents of OPEN twice as much as was charged in Managua, the people immediately formed the "Coordinating Committee for the Defense of Water" and encouraged everyone to resist paying the high price. There were demonstrations and vast assemblies. Leaflets were distributed and placards carried which read, "We will not pay the price until it is lowered to ten cordobas." The Somoza-affiliated water company waged its own campaign with loudspeakers and fliers to discredit the challengers. The National Guard prevented all demonstrations in the streets. While the censorship of the press kept the story from being carried in the local papers, the people of OPEN sent a letter to all of the parishes of Managua telling the story and asking for support as they struggled against "one further step in the repression."

During the week of July 4, 1976, when the United States was celebrating its two hundredth birthday, Maura wrote to her parents, "I enjoyed hearing about the Bicentennial and the beautiful tall ships. We had planned a get together for a special celebration but it wasn't possible as we are having a big campaign here in the barrio about the price of water. Pray for this intention, that the poor do not suffer but gain a little something from this."[5] The protest continued for the next four months, during which Maura went one step further in her understanding of what it means to serve the poor by standing with them and resisting oppression rather than merely dealing with its effects.

When the National Guard broke up a peaceful demonstration in OPEN and, as had become routine, attempted to carry some of the youths to prison, where they would be interrogated or tortured or would simply disappear, Maura surprised her neighbors, the Sisters, the National Guard, and herself by banging on the hood of the military Jeep with her fist and crying, "You may not take these young men! Let them go!"

They did let them go, and that moment is still remembered by the people of OPEN as one of courage and hope. If one as full of peace as Maura could defeat the National Guard, they thought, then what could they do if they were courageous and united?

Maura had known for some time that she would be returning to Maryknoll, New York, in the fall of 1976 to work in one of the congregational offices for three years. "Leaving Nicaragua is going to be hard," she wrote to her parents. "These are such good and wonderful people and I care for them so much."[6]

Soon after returning to the United States, Maura received reports of the continuing "water fight" and learned of the death of the leaders of the Sandinista Front for National Liberation (FSLN) and the disappearance of at least 350 *campesinos* around Siuna. During an eight-day retreat she prayed about those events and wrote her thoughts in a notebook.

> I entered into a time of sadness and deep loneliness and wept over my separation from the people I love, the Sisters, Fathers, all. I saw the tortured people who fight for justice today in the place of Christ, and I pictured the rulers and the military as the high priests. I envisioned the poor, Ricardo, Asuncion, Dionisio, as the tortured Jesus.[7]

Even though Maura longed to be in Nicaragua at that important point in the history of the people she loved, or perhaps precisely because she was still with them, she immersed herself in the work of conducting "World Awareness Programs," workshops on the missionary work of the Church in Third World countries. She believed her work to be "a channel for awakening real concern for the victims in today's world, a means to work for change and to awaken deep concern for the sufferings of the poor and marginated, the non-persons of our human family."[8]

CHAPTER 10

Solidarity

In January 1978, after giving several world awareness programs to parish and teachers' groups in the Boston area, Maura and her partner, Sister Jennie Burke, a native of Boston with mission experience in Hawaii, were invited to work full-time for a year in the Boston Archdiocese. They accepted, though Maura felt inadequate, unable to quote statistics or analyze the intricacies of political ideologies at work in the lives of the people she loved. Instead, she spoke from her heart of her seventeen years experience in Nicaragua.

In September 1978, during a rally called to protest United States' aid to Somoza's government, Maura was asked to speak in place of a political science expert who had canceled at the last minute. Maura looked around her at the hundreds of people, swallowed her lack of self-confidence, and climbed the stairs of the courthouse.

She spoke of the natural beauty of Nicaragua, the goodness of the people, of their need and strength. She spoke of the repression, of the wealth shared among Somoza and a few of his friends, of the misery and malnutrition of the people Maura knew as neighbors. She told the crowd that the people of Nicaragua wanted nothing more than a decent life and reason to hope in the future and their children's future. And she assured those present that the people would rid themselves of their dictator because they had become strong by working together. Then she asked those in attendance to urge Congress and President Carter to recognize the just struggle of the Nicaraguan people, to support democratic movements rather than "friendly dictatorships," and to work to develop more equitable relationships among nations. The applause was loud and long.

Between programs or whenever her schedule allowed, Maura was at Maryknoll. She was there one evening in the fall of 1978 when Sisters Marie Estelle Coupe and Peg Dillon, delegates from

Nicaragua to the Maryknoll Sisters Eleventh General Assembly, gave their report on the history and most recent developments of the conflict. She heard firsthand how Peg Dillon, from Hamburg, New York, Julianne Warnshuis from Los Angeles, and the Spanish Jesuit priest Father Benigno Fernandez were knocked down and clubbed with rifle butts when they tried to keep the National Guard from arresting students during a peaceful demonstration in OPEN. She heard the story of Julie Miller and Pat Murray, from Brooklyn, who had been picked up in Tola when they tried to prevent the National Guard from taking their parish priest after Mass one Sunday morning. And she listened as Estelle described the aftermath of the assassination of the courageous editor of *La Prensa*, Pedro Joaquin Chamorro, and of the 50,000 frightened but determined people who accompanied his body in the seven hour pre-funeral procession. "You can't assassinate them all!" *La Prensa* boldly proclaimed the following day. She listened with gratitude and hope to the clear stand the Church was taking and was heartened to hear that the bishops of Nicaragua had strongly denounced the outrageous dictatorship of Somoza as illegitimate.

As the Sisters' Assembly progressed, national television, the press, and personal correspondence were full of the violence in Nicaragua. This served as a dramatic illustration of what was happening in varying degrees throughout the world and helped clarify the community's mission, convictions and vision for the next six years.

Ita Ford was also at Maryknoll during the Assembly, often skipping her theology classes to attend the open sessions. On more than one occasion she was invited to assist in editing papers for various committees. She was proud to be asked to edit the Mission Vision statement, which both captures and inspires the spirit of the congregation as perceived by that assembly. "The salvific mission of the poor is becoming visible to the Church and offering hope to our world," the statement reads in part. "Solidarity with the poor is not an option but a sign of the Kingdom that must be made explicit in our day. We commit ourselves to the cause of the poor through the witness of our lives, our word and our ministry."[1]

During the Thanksgiving holidays, Estelle Coupe visited her family in Cumberland, Rhode Island, and, in spite of her family's misgivings, had been characteristically outspoken during an interview with the diocesan newspaper. She told of National Guard brutality, of the Church's stand with the people against Somoza, and delivered the message entrusted to her by Bishop Manuel Salazar, President of the Nicaraguan Catholic Bishops' Conference. "Tell the people of the United States," he urged, "that we are fighting for freedom and ask them to support us with a hands-off policy."[2]

Earlier, in an interview with WOR Radio in New York City, she had spoken of the United States government's support of the hated Somoza family, of the Church's role in bringing the people of Nicaragua to an awareness of their dignity, and of the consequent turmoil following decades of oppression. Though Estelle had requested that neither interview be made public until she was safely back in Nicaragua, one was broadcast and the other published on November 12 and 28, two weeks before she left the United States.

On December 14, Estelle flew to Texas to meet Sister Patricia Nolan, a Brooklynite who was visiting with her family there and with whom she would be traveling to Nicaragua by Jeep. Just a day into their journey, near the town of Saltillo, Mexico, on a well-paved though lonesome four-lane divided highway, something occurred that perhaps will never be explained. On Sunday morning, December 16, the State Department called Maryknoll to tell of the accident the day before that left Patricia Nolan with multiple fractures and Estelle in a coma. When the Maryknoll Sisters in Mexico arrived at the little hospital, the nurses told them that Pat had repeated over and over again, "Be careful, Estelle, they're trying to push us off the road!"[3]

"We have not been able to get any details of just how the accident happened," a letter from Maryknoll informed the Sisters throughout the world. "Although one woman said she had seen the Sisters before the accident occurred, no eyewitness has come forward to give us any information. Any effort to get information, so far, has failed."[4] Estelle never regained consciousness, and Pat has no recollection of those terrible moments.

Maura went for a long walk through the woods when the news of the accident was received at Maryknoll, and then she sat for awhile on a bench at the edge of the cemetery. Estelle was flown to New York within a few weeks and admitted to the Sisters' nursing home, where Maura visited her whenever she was there. She would pray with her, holding her hand and talking with her as she always had, telling what news had been received of their friends and the events in Nicaragua. Though the Sisters and nurses were not quite sure how to explain it, they claimed that Estelle seemed to respond whenever Maura spoke to her.

The tragic news was felt throughout the Maryknoll world, especially by those women who had been with Estelle only days before in New York and those who had known her over the years in Hawaii, Nicaragua, and Chile.

Estelle had gone to Chile only months before and had become acquainted with the country under Pinochet—so changed from the Chile she had known. Until that visit, Carla had remembered Estelle only as the proper superior who had reprimanded her for writing "Dear Guillermo" to the bishop in 1964. Fourteen years later, however, Carla had been impressed by Estelle's commitment to the struggling people of Nicaragua and her tears over what had become of Chile.

Carla and Connie had received letters from Ita in New York in which she mentioned Estelle's courage in attempting to clarify what was happening in Nicaragua, and later "shuddered" at the news of the accident. More than that, Carla was angry—angry at whatever it is that cannot live with the truth. It was just one more thing, one major thing, to drag her farther and farther down into a heavy restlessness that she had felt since Ita left.

She seemed unable to be sure of anyone's affection or respect for her, and occasionally a misunderstanding or simple difference of opinion would be alienating. During that year of Ita's absence, Connie remembered, "Carla felt a dimming of her creativity and desperately clung to the Bible as she felt her faith slipping out from under her feet."[5]

For several years Carla had been going once a month to the Benedictine monastery outside the city of Santiago for a day of prayer and fasting and to talk with her confessor. As life became increasingly difficult and empty, she went more often, and yet she never seemed to find the peace for which she longed—the peace, perhaps, she had never truly known.

She began to see La Bandera as a desert, a barren waste where everything refused to grow, where life was infinitely dry and hopeless. Saplings, in fact, had begun to grow and to provide some green and shade in the dusty yards of the neighborhood, and people cared for whatever flowers appeared. But Carla was not speaking of plants; she was projecting the hue of her own hopes and dreams and creativity onto the world around her. La Bandera was truly a desert.

Irritable and restless, Carla knew the time had come for her to move again, but Ita was due to return within a few months and she would wait until then to make her decision.

CHAPTER 11

A Poor Old Beggar

The year of study and prayer at Maryknoll, New York, had strengthened Ita's dedication to mission, though she had become more detached than ever about making final vows, the step toward which reflection year was directed. During her retreat in May 1979, Ita expressed her position in a written evaluation.

> I don't relate to final commitment, she wrote, except as a canonical requirement. My own history within Maryknoll probably shapes this attitude. By the time I made my commitment in 1972, I had been through an 11 year period of clarifying what my call was and how it should be expressed. Being reasonably sure myself and more confident in God's faithfulness, my commitment was for my life. Since then, many different experiences have helped flesh out and make this choice clearer and more meaningful. I believe I am responding to the Lord's call to me in the best way through the means of Maryknoll, cooperating in the Church's evangelizing mission to the poor and the oppressed and living simply in a celibate community. This is where my life has meaning, challenge, and fulfillment. Besides, I'm happy and I like it. I'll be glad to fulfill the final requirement on my return to Chile.[1]

The next day some friends picked up Ita at the rest and retreat house in Watch Hill, Rhode Island, on their way to Massachusetts to spend one last weekend together before Ita's departure. It was dark by the time they were on the main road just fifteen minutes from Watch Hill, and no one saw clearly what happened. It seemed that a car traveling in the opposite direction suddenly swung around and crashed into the left rear door, hitting Ita. Then it drove on.

"Don't move her! It may be her back," warned one of Ita's three unharmed friends.

Taken by ambulance to a hospital, Ita insisted on calling her mother herself. She had to remain there for a month with a broken pelvis and torn knee. The doctor was amazed at her constant exercising and stubborn determination to get through the period of tedious recovery in order to return to Chile. Father John Patrick Meehan visited her at the house in Watch Hill when she was released from the hospital. "I thought the accident would put her into a depressed state," he remembered, "but I learned that if anything her spirit was even more at peace. Her prayer grew deeper and she seemed to understand that this too was part of her preparation for something. She looked on her convalescence as a great time of prayer and peace, a truly gifted time."[2]

Yet Ita's tendency to wrestle playfully with God was still there. "Who's in control? Who's in charge here? have been questions in the dialogue I've been involved in during these days at Watch Hill," she wrote to Rachel Lauze.

> I don't know why it's such a struggle, that there are so many levels of letting go, but I keep coming up against it a lot. I wouldn't volunteer for a car accident but I guess we just manage as things come along. Wisdom of my venerable Chinese grandmother: expect the unexpected.[3]

On May 25, 1979, the day of Ita's accident, Julie Miller was traveling from her new mission in La Libertad, El Salvador, through Nicaragua to a meeting in Panama. While she was with the Sisters in Leon, Nicaragua, the final offensive against Somoza began, and there she remained for the duration of the war.

In La Bandera one day in early June, the Sisters received further news of the war in Nicaragua and prayed and worried about their friends there. During supper, Connie told Carla that she was thinking of offering to go to Nicaragua for awhile, that perhaps one of the Sisters might need a rest from the situation for a month or two. Carla, who had been more upset than ever since receiving the news of Ita's accident and delayed return, immediately decided that she too would offer to go.

The next morning they consulted with their regional governing board in Chile and then called Maryknoll, New York. Everyone encouraged them to go if they could get in.

They tried reaching Nicaragua by phone, sent cables, mailed letters, went to the United States Embassy in Santiago and to the Red Cross. They tried everything they could think of, but could not get through. The raging conflict, it seemed, had effectively cut off all normal means of communication with the outside world. Julie and six other Sisters in Leon found themselves running a spontaneously organized refugee center for 400 people with 20 cots, a small supply of rice, beans, medicines, and 5,000 gallons of water. Their only contact with the world beyond the boundaries of Nicaragua was an occasional brave reporter through whom they were able to send letters assuring family and friends of their safety while trying to camouflage their fear. One reporter, Bill Gentile from ABC and UPI, called President Somoza when he returned to Managua from Leon to tell him that if anything happened to the seven North American Sisters in the refugee center in Leon, he would make sure it received worldwide publicity. "If they don't bother us," Somoza assured him, "we won't bother them."[4]

In New York City, Maura Clarke had been invited to join in a fast at Riverside Church, one of many events being organized throughout the country to pray for the peace and freedom of the Nicaraguan people. "I don't know if I can do it,"[5] she confided to friends, but she did. Two days later, on July 17, Somoza, defeated, finally left Nicaragua. Maura cried as if released from pain. She was full of both joy and sadness. She wrote to the Sisters in Nicaragua:

> I feel so proud of you, so full of awe and wonder at what you have suffered and witnessed. It is incredible and yet it is true. What can I say? Somehow you have all taken on a new strangeness—special, heroic—and I fear not being able to relate to you, that you are different, changed, not the same Sisters of mine that I know after all you've been through and endured and learned to believe.
>
> Maybe I am sad in a way to be left out of all that you have experienced. And yet for some reason the Lord wanted it this way. I think that you should be there and I here with you in spirit and love and prayer.[6]

That message, never sent, was found in a notebook after Maura's death.

On July 17, Ita wrote to Rachel Lauze from Watch Hill, Rhode Island, "Today I especially missed the old group. After a year of talking, praying, being wrapped up in Nicaragua, it was so strange not to be together when Somoza finally left. I pray that true peace can be made now by those who are left behind to rebuild."[7]

In Chile's La Bandera, Carla and Connie were relieved when they heard the news of Somoza's defeat and wondered if their letters had ever been received. Carla was more anxious than ever to go to Nicaragua and just as ready to leave La Bandera. Her friend, Sister Rebecca Quinn, a Philadelphian with twenty-six years experience in Chile, was alone in the southern town of Coelemu and, knowing Carla needed a change, invited her to come for a couple of months. Perhaps during that time she might receive word from Nicaragua and Ita might be ready to return.

In Nicaragua, the Sisters from Leon, OPEN, and Condega were preparing to go to Costa Rica for the vacation they had fantasized in an attempt to maintain their spirits during the war and to plan for the future. They reported how grateful they were to have been present with the people of Nicaragua in their hours of anguish and triumph. And yet they knew,

> The task before us is gigantic for the real revolution begins now, the revolution against hunger, corruption, ignorance, individualism, disease, selfishness and greed. As Maryknoll Sisters we have a unique opportunity to continue to build the Kingdom of Justice, Peace and Friendship side by side within the revolution whose ideals echo those of the Gospel.[8]

To Connie and Carla they wrote, "Yes, do come, but plan on staying for a year or two." Connie's work in Chile made such a long-term "loan" impossible. Carla would go sometime after Christmas, after Ita's return.

When Carla left La Bandera to go to Coelemu, she gave away almost everything she owned except what books and clothes would fit in a shopping bag. "The Lord is calling me to be poor with his poor," were her parting words, almost as if she had never said them before.

"Here I am in Coelemu with Becky," Carla wrote to Connie.

"Bandera was getting to me and now I'm glad I'm here. This place is a small city but surrounded by rolling hills that lift the drooping spirit. I thank God I have this memory of Chile as I prepare to go North."[9]

She was delighted with her "bedroom," which consisted of a cot in the hallway of a widow's house where Becky had rented two rooms. To mark the turn in her life, she bought pastel patches of material which she asked a neighbor to sew into a "rainbow dress," the only dress she would take to Nicaragua.

Though Ita's principal task for the summer was to exercise and get well, there was plenty of time in between for odd jobs such as translating, editing, and writing letters. All the while, she was quietly thinking about the future. During the entire past year, both the war in Nicaragua and the increasingly courageous voice of Archbishop Oscar Romero in El Salvador drew Ita's attention to Central America. As requests for personnel continued to come from Archbishop Romero and the Church in Nicaragua, Sisters with Latin American experience—especially those who were between jobs—were asked to consider an assignment to either of those countries. If Ita decided to go, she knew it would be to El Salvador, not only because there were fewer Sisters there but because, unlike Nicaragua, El Salvador was still suffering from terrible repression. More influential in her decision, perhaps, was the fact that the archbishop's understanding of the mission of the Church was that of "accompanying" the people as they struggled to live fully human lives under oppression. This view of mission inspired Ita and echoed what she had come to understand in Chile.

"The challenge that we live daily is to enter into the paschal mystery with faith," Ita had written in 1977. "Am I willing to suffer with the people here, the suffering of the powerless? Can I say to my neighbors, 'I have no solution to this situation; I don't know the answers, but I will walk with you, search with you, be with you'?"[10]

One night in October, Julie Miller called Ita at Maryknoll, New York, from Nicaragua to check on her travel plans. During the brief call Ita mentioned what she had been secretly thinking. "No, not you, Ita. Not El Salvador after the Chile coup and now this accident. We'll talk when you come."[11]

By November the doctor was pleased by the progress Ita had made but warned her to avoid those countries where she might have to run. She laughed, packed her duffle bag, and walked without a limp through the front door of Maryknoll, where the Sisters had gathered with noisemakers and hugs for the traditional departure.

"When Ita came to Nicaragua in November of 1979," Julie recalled, "after her accident and my war, we were all in bed when she came over to me, took my hand and started to cry. I asked her what was wrong and she said, 'You're alive.' I got up and we went outside and talked for several hours."[12]

And though they talked for the next few days about the possibility of going to El Salvador, both Ita and Julie knew that no decision would be made until Ita returned to Chile.

In Santiago, after spending a day and a night with the Sisters there, Ita boarded a train that took her south to Coelemu, where Carla met her at the station, her T-shirt painted with butterflies and the simple message, "Welcome home, Ita."

They went to the beach for several days with Becky Quinn to catch up on the past year and a half. Carla told of how unexpected a gift that time in Coelemu had been and how happy she would be to stay there if she had not already decided to go to Nicaragua. "But then," she said, "when you hold onto things that make you happy they have the tendency to fade and crumble."[13]

On January 14, 1980, wearing her rainbow dress and carrying one small suitcase, Carla said good-bye to her friends in Chile. In a letter to her sister, Betty, and brother-in-law Jack, she tried to capture the meaning of this move to Nicaragua.

So many times in my life I have had to give up something very precious only to be gifted with something else I never dreamed of asking for but received in my poorness with great gratitude and lately with joy. When I left La Bandera I was quite dead in many ways. I went to the south to work in a mission where I didn't even have a room but rather slept in the hall, and since the other Sister and I were only renting a room we had to eat with the priests, which I can't say I enjoy. However, I came to love the work so much that even the priests weren't hard to take and by the time I left I enjoyed them as good brothers with whom I could joke and fight and really learn from. I learned a story here in Coelemu which I would like to share.

One day an old beat-up beggar was walking along the road

with only a pocketful of grain for his daily fare. He thought within himself, "If only the King would pass by, I could receive something and be filled."

As he walked he noticed in the distance that a carriage was coming and he got all excited since he realized it was the King. He knelt by the side of the road and the King stopped and went over to the beggar and held out his hand. The beggar was confused when the King continued to hold out his hand and say, "What have you to give me?" The beggar said, "But I'm a beggar, poor and needy. What can I give you?" The King only smiled and continued to hold out his hand. The beggar reached into his pocket and gave the King one kernel of his pocketful of grain. The King took it and continued on his journey.

The poor ole beat-up beggar continued on his way and in the evening, in his shack, took out his grain to eat before lying down to sleep. He emptied his pocket on the table and noticed that among the kernels, one was gold. He looked through all of them but only noticed one kernel of solid gold. Then he recalled the kernel he had given the King and sighed, "Why didn't I give him all?"

Many times I have been as the beggar, giving one little kernel . . . when I left Chile, I can truly say I gave all that I knew at the time—friends, work, even culture and the history of a people I had grown to love and appreciate—yet I believe that Our Father is so generous and loving, He'll do even more and be more in Nicaragua or El Salvador—wherever I end up.[14]

Back in Santiago, Ita was weighing the pros and cons of going to El Salvador or remaining in Chile. During the next several weeks, she visited the twelve Maryknoll Sister houses in the country, spoke with each of the Sisters at length, and in La Bandera, kept Connie up way into the night for nights on end. Ironically, the strongest thing holding her back was the fact that Carla would be practically next door in Nicaragua. In her always meticulous sorting out of motives, Ita had to be certain and free in her own mind and heart that her commitment to the Church's mission in El Salvador was sufficiently compelling in itself to seal her decision to go. She was close enough to the decision, however, to introduce the idea to her mother.

> One thing I wanted to share has been in the air since last September and is still there though it should be taking shape in a month or so. Around the time of my knee operation, I began to get interested in El Salvador and I talked to Regina McEvoy of our Central Governing Board a couple of times... I've had to look at that priority and say I'm open to consider it. It's very important at this time to support Archbishop Romero ... Pray with me that I make the right decision when the time comes. I'll let you know as it develops.[15]

Meanwhile, Carla arrived in Nicaragua and wrote enthusiastically of all that was happening as the people began rebuilding their country and their lives following the defeat of Somoza. She wrote of the many priests, religious, and lay Christians who were participating in the National Literacy Crusade, a valiant and largely successful attempt to incorporate all Nicaraguans into the revolutionary process by eliminating illiteracy. "It really is exciting to experience,"[16] Carla reported.

The sacrifices made for victory were visible too.

> On Wednesday I observed and felt the horrible ravages of the war. I dedicated myself to looking at the faces of these people where the hope and conviction of building up a new society are mirrored. In the evening as I went over to Ocotal in the truck the driver began to tell a bit of what it was like in Condega. As he told of the atrocities of the National Guard and of how they came in and tortured and killed entire families, he began to cry while we were on those curvy mountain roads. It was one of those experiences that are recorded forever.[17]

Some of the Sisters who were actually assigned to El Salvador had been "caught" by the final offensive in Nicaragua and unable to leave the country during the last several weeks of the war. Those Sisters, including Julie Miller, decided to remain in Nicaragua to help the people with whom they had lived through the violence and the terror. The alternative would be to return to El Salvador, where they were not quite sure they could endure another war. So it was that only two Sisters remained in El Salvador, a fact that shifted the weight of concern to that mission country.

Top to Bottom:
Ita Ford,
Carla Piette,
Maura Clarke.

Ita Ford, high school graduation;

as a postulant with her brother, Bill (1962);

with Bill's children (1979).

Maura Clarke, age four;
as a college freshman, 1959;
in Nicaragua;
in the late 1970s.

Carla and Ita in Chile.

Ita and Carla (far left and far right) with other Maryknoll Sisters;

Ita and Maura Clarke in El Salvador;

Ita in El Salvador.

Archbishop Oscar Romero
of San Salvador.

Lay missioner Jean Donovan and Ursuline Sister
Dorothy Kazel in El Salvador, 1980.

Below, the last photo taken of Ita and Maura
with other Maryknoll Sisters attending a meeting
in Managua.

Susan Meiselas

The discovery of the bodies.

Below, the graves of Ita, Carla, and Maura in El Salvador.

CHAPTER 12

A Shepherd's Sacrifice

El Salvador, a naturally beautiful little country of 4.5 million people, is one of the most densely populated nations in the Third World. In 1932 the military government of General Maximiliano Hernandez Martinez massacred 30,000 peasants when they rose up against the military, which had overthrown the civilian government the year before. The military continued to rule, protecting the interests of 2 percent of the population, an oligarchy of 14 extended families.

In the 1960s several political parties were formed in a movement toward democracy, and in 1972 and 1977 they were strong enough to compete in the presidential elections. When massive fraud resulted in military victories in both elections, many peasants and urban workers lost all faith in the electoral process and joined together in mass popular movements. To counter those groups, the military government and wealthy families built up "anti-terrorist" death squads, the most famous of which was ORDEN. The death squads also operated against labor and peasant leaders, Catholic Church personnel taking prominent roles in defense of human rights, and local political leaders sympathetic to the popular movements. In 1979 Napoleon Duarte became president by means of a coup that was rumored to have been orchestrated in Washington. While outspoken Archbishop Oscar Romero expressed only tentative support for the new government and strongly opposed all United States military aid used to repress the people, the United States gave its support to the "moderate and centrist" government and immediately approved the resumption of military supplies. As the violence increased, so did the requests from the Archdiocese of San Salvador for Church personnel to accompany the victims of the repression.

During an area meeting in Managua, Nicaragua, shortly after

Carla's arrival, in February 1980, the Sisters spoke of the personnel shortage in the neighboring country of El Salvador. "Since I'm in the looking around stage," Carla wrote, "I offered to go with the idea of seeing what we could do and then present this to the Sisters."[1]

"Zipping" through Nicaragua and Honduras to El Salvador in buses that Carla nicknamed "microwave ovens since they average 90 to 100 degrees," Carla immediately felt the difference between Nicaragua and "this concentrated little bouillon cube of a country"[2] where violence, revenge, poverty, and wealth were all in the extreme. Stories of mutilated bodies being found were constant; fear was epidemic. The smell of poverty was overpowering in the dark little hovels in Santa Ana she visited with Sister Madeline Dorsey. The elegant resort hotels (underpopulated, to be sure) along the deserted Pacific beaches were bizarre and even obscene in the context of such misery and violence. Carla listened to Archbishop Romero's homilies by radio and realized the hope and love he stirred in the hearts of the people. When she saw him, "his great holiness and love for the truth"[3] impressed her. She wrote of other first impressions in a letter to the Sisters in Chile.

> Actually, I don't find El Salvador all that different from Chile, except that there is obvious armed resistance from the people to the National Security State repression.[4]
>
> I like this place with its spunky people. If this country had had the democratic government that Chile had for so long, El Salvador would be the most developed country in the world. I've never seen such an energetic crowd. Even road gangs really work. I call them little ants, always on the run, selling things or fixing their houses or cleaning. I can't keep up with them. But given their history and the people who have had the power, they just make ends meet and now the top is about to blow off—and with reason.[5]

Carla quickly came to the decision to work in El Salvador but returned to Nicaragua to finalize the assignment with the Sisters there.

In La Bandera, meanwhile, Ita was composing a letter to her mother.

The last week or two have been spent mostly letting the El Salvador possibility roll around inside me. I went to the new house of prayer and what I came to and feel good with is the decision to go. I realize this isn't the greatest news I've ever given you and, in fact, one of the cons was that the family would not be overjoyed, but I think it's a good decision. I'll also be a continent nearer![6]

In Managua, Nicaragua, on March 17, the Sisters were celebrating St. Patrick's Day when Ita called from Chile. "Julie, Carla, are you both there? I just want to tell you that I'm coming to El Salvador."

In New York, Maura Clarke had finished her three years on the Mission Education team and was giving much thought to her approaching return to Nicaragua. She wrote:

This past year will never be forgotten by the Nicaraguans and all those who love them because they have come to the beginning of a new freedom and have suffered much pain and death in order to bring forth new life and hope, not only for their own children, but for other Latin Americans.[7]

And yet, since El Salvador has been made a priority for Sisters with some Latin American experience I may be going there. This I must pray about and discern so that I will not be naive and go on superficial motivation, but by what the Lord wishes only.[8]

El Salvador was much in the news in the Spring of 1980, not only because of the violence but because of the outspoken peacefulness of San Salvador's Archbishop Oscar Romero. Every Sunday morning during Mass in the Cathedral in San Salvador, his sermons, which lasted about one hour and a half, were broadcast by the archdiocesan radio station, YSAX. Every Sunday morning 73 percent of the rural population and 47 percent of the urban population listened as their archbishop told, in concrete terms, of the suffering of entire communities of Christians, of the violence from the repressive right and the left, never ceasing to call for peace and reconciliation as he preached the Word of God as hope for the poor.

Neither Archbishop Romero's pastoral vision nor his homilies were the creation of one person. From the young man who organized the information that came into the archdiocesan office and clipped newspaper articles each day, to the rural communities that sent messengers into San Salvador with accounts of the latest violence, to the people of the chancery legal aid office who gathered and circulated information about missing persons and labor problems and inquired about the fate of prisoners, to the team of people who compiled it all—the Christian community of El Salvador composed the archbishop's Sunday sermons. And neither was the pastoral stance of "accompanying" the people the vision of one person but was shared by most pastoral personnel in his diocese. For that reason, when he was named to receive an honorary doctorate from the University of Louvain, Belgium, in February 1980, though he personally felt it was something like being "in a Miss Universe contest," Archbishop Romero accepted the honor in the name of the people of El Salvador.

In his acceptance speech he said,

> I am a shepherd who, with his people, has begun to learn a beautiful and difficult truth: our Christian faith requires that we submerge ourselves in this world.
>
> The course taken by the Church has always had political repercussions. The problem is how to direct that influence so that it will be in accord with the faith.
>
> The world that the Church must serve is the world of the poor, and the poor are the ones who decide what it means for the Church to really live in the world. . .
>
> It is the poor who force us to understand what is really taking place . . . the persecution of the Church is a result of defending the poor. Our persecution is nothing more nor less than sharing in the destiny of the poor. The poor are the Body of Christ today. Through them He lives on in history . . .[9]

On February 17, 1980, after reading an article about United States military aid to El Salvador, Archbishop Romero sent an open and widely publicized letter to President Jimmy Carter.

> In the past few days news has appeared in the national press that worries me greatly, news that the government of the United States is studying a form of abetting the arming of El Salvador by sending military teams and advisors to "train

three Salvadoran battalions in logistics, communications and intelligence." If this information from the newspapers is correct, the contribution of your government, instead of promoting greater justice and peace in El Salvador, will without doubt sharpen the injustice and repression against the organizations of the people who repeatedly have been struggling to gain respect for their most fundamental human rights.[10]

The archbishop pointed out that the government then in power was even more repressive than the one before, which had been denounced by the Inter-American Committee on Human Rights. He pleaded with President Carter,

> I ask you, if you truly want to defend human rights, to prohibit the giving of this military aid to the Salvadoran government. Guarantee that your government will not intervene directly or indirectly . . . It would be unjust and deplorable if the intrusion of foreign powers were to frustrate the Salvadoran people, were to repress them and block their autonomous decisions about the economic and political path that our country ought to follow. It would violate a right which we Latin American bishops meeting in Puebla publicly recognized when we said, "The legitimate self-determination of our people permits them to organize according to their own genius and the march of their history and to cooperate in a new international order."[11]

In the last days of February, in an interview with a reporter of the Mexican newspaper *Excelsior*, Archbishop Romero spoke what seems now to have been prophecy but was only a realistic assessment of the forces against him.

> My life has been threatened many times. I have to confess that as a Christian, I don't believe in death without resurrection. If they kill me, I will rise again in the Salvadoran people.
>   As a shepherd I am obliged by divine law to give my life for those I love, for the entire Salvadoran people, including those Salvadorans who threaten to assassinate me. If they should go so far as to carry out their threats, I want you to

know that I now offer my blood to God for justice and the resurrection of El Salvador.

Martyrdom is a grace of God that I do not feel worthy of. But if God accepts the sacrifice of my life, my hope is that my blood will be like a seed of liberty and a sign that our hopes will soon become reality.[12]

Churches, human rights organizations, and solidarity groups throughout the world were becoming increasingly aware of the situation in Central America because of the fame of El Salvador's courageous archbishop. Letters of support poured into the archbishop's office and were answered. On March 18, 1980, Sister Melinda Roper, president of the Maryknoll Sisters, received a response to a letter she had written the archbishop a few weeks before.

I want to express my deepest gratitude to you and your congregation for your beautiful letter of solidarity with our local Church in its task of being one with the suffering people of El Salvador.

Your religious family with whom we feel united both physically and through prayer, reaffirms once again our position of complete dedication to the work of the Kingdom of the life of Christ which has its basis in the large number of the poor, in order to call the powerful from their position to conversion.

I pray that you will extend to all the Maryknoll Sisters all the pastoral affection of my greeting and blessing.[13]

Less than a week later, on Sunday, March 23, 1980, after a worse than typical week of violence and death, Archbishop Romero explained again, lest there be any listeners still unable to understand, why he spoke of politics and temporal matters when preaching the Word of God.

I have tried during these Sundays of Lent to keep uncovering—in the divine revelation contained in the Word that is read here at Mass—God's program to save peoples and individuals. Today, when our people stand at the crossroads of history, we can say surely that the way that best reflects God's program will win out. This is the Church's mission. In the light of God's Word revealing God's plan for the happiness of peoples, we have the duty of pointing out also the realities, of seeing how God's plan is reflected among us or despised among us. Let no one take it ill that in the light of God's words read in our Mass we enlighten social, political, and economic realities. If we did not, it would not be Christianity for us. It is thus that Christ willed to become incarnate, so that the light that he brings from the Father may become the life of persons and of nations.[14]

After recalling the long list of atrocities that occurred during the previous week, Romero spoke of the government.

If it intends to behead the people's organization and block the political development that the people want, no other program can succeed. Without roots in the people, no government can avail, much less so when it wants to impose its program through bloodshed and sorrow.

I would like to make an appeal in a special way to the men of the army, and in particular to the ranks of the *Guardia Nacional,* of the police, to those in the barracks. Brothers, you are part of our own people. You kill your own campesino brothers and sisters. And before an order to kill that a man may give, the law of God must prevail that says, "Thou shalt not kill!" No soldier is obliged to obey an order against the law of God. No one has to fulfill an immoral law. It is time to recover your consciences and to obey your consciences rather than the order of sin. The Church, defender of the rights of God, of human dignity, the dignity of the person, cannot remain silent before such an abomination. We want the government to take seriously that reforms are worth nothing when they come about stained with so much blood. In the name of God, and in the name of this suffering people whose laments rise to heaven each day more tumultuous, I beg you, I ask you, I order you in the name of God: Stop the repression![15]

The applause in the cathedral was thundering.
The next day, March 24, 1980, at 6:25 in the evening, just as he

finished the homily of the Mass for the mother of a friend in the chapel of the Hospital of Divine Providence where he lived in a simple little house, Archbishop Oscar Arnulfo Romero was shot and killed.

A few moments after six that same evening, Carla arrived in San Salvador by bus from Nicaragua and, together with Sisters Madeline (Maddie) Dorsey, originally from Brooklyn, and Joan Petrik, from Baltimore, drove the two and one-half hours to Santa Ana by Jeep. "It was close to nine o'clock Monday evening when we arrived in Santa Ana," Joan remembered.

> Things did not appear to be normal and, upon investigating in the community, Maddie was told that the Archbishop had been killed. She came back shocked, told us about it and we all sat stunned. We went into chapel and prayed. When we turned on the radio and T.V. we were enraged to find stations continuing their regular programs. We had to get a Nicaraguan station for the news about his death.[16]

The next morning they returned to San Salvador. "Here I am sitting on the steps of the Basilica of the Sacred Heart in San Salvador where the body of Archbishop Romero has been brought in silent procession," Carla wrote to Sister Regina McEvoy at Maryknoll, New York.

> The sadness that slowly settles over a people at the death of a father, pastor, guide, and prophet is the sadness that Salvador is now wrapped in. It was said the night of his death that Romero was killed by injustice, the hatred and the lies which he so valiantly denounced. How many times, it was recalled, he begged, supplicated and repeated, "Do not kill!" With banners repeating the simple statement the archbishop's body was carried to the cathedral . . .[17]

While she was in the basilica, Carla's passport was stolen, so she spent the next several days going back and forth to the American embassy.

> It's full of buzzers, searchers, guards, bars and gloom, such a contrast to the way in which the archbishop had lived, so

simply, for the poor and for truth, with no guards, and the
Lord blessed him with the greatest likeness to Jesus—giving
his life for the poor. I'm praying for the conversion of the
USA.[18]

During the week-long wake, Carla went each day

to the Basilica for Mass and unworthily was privileged to be
in the guard of honor for this saintly man. As I stood before
his body I prayed that I might be converted also from my
pride and egoism to be of the *pueblo* as I watched the masses
file by and cry with me—I believe I am being healed. I
believe that this country is being healed at the high price of
blood and lives. I am really glad to be here and I believe it is
where we should be.[19]

On Palm Sunday, the day of the funeral, Church dignitaries of
all denominations from Europe, the United States, and Latin America came to pay their respects to this man of peace. They joined
thousands of people in the Palm Sunday procession as Monseñor
Oscar Romero's remains were reverently carried the ten blocks
from Sacred Heart Basilica to the cathedral. Occupied for weeks in
silent prayerful protest of the repression, the cathedral was respect-
fully disoccupied for the burial Mass. Because of the thousands of
people who gathered, Mass was celebrated on the cathedral steps.
"The priests and Sisters sat inside the cathedral behind the altar,"
the Sisters remembered vividly.

The visiting prelates, clergy, and ecumenical groups were
around the altar on the steps of the cathedral and the laity
filled the streets and the plaza in front of the cathedral and to
the side of the national palace.
    The four men representing the leadership of the popular
organizations (which are often erroneously labeled "subversive communist groups") reached the plaza during the homily. It was interesting to note the respect of this huge compact
crowd for the coordinating committee. They automatically
opened a path for them as they took their place in front of the
cathedral steps and passed a huge wreath forward to be placed
near the coffin. It was at this very moment, the climax of the

homily and the moment of tribute of the popular groups to
this man of peace, that all violence broke out.[20]

Bombs and gunfire lasted for forty-five minutes as thousands of
people ran in all directions. Some reached the packed security of
the cathedral. Others fell and were trampled or died by bullets. "It
was good for all of us," the Sisters concluded, "to experience with
the people the danger and fear and anger of being subjected to
violence."[21]

That evening, when the Sisters met to pray, they read St. Luke's
account of the appearance of the two sorrowing disciples as they
walked to Emmaus. The Sisters later wrote:

> Like those two disciples, our Easter joy was not joyous. We
> have recognized the Lord but not really seen him yet in total
> liberation. We feel he has told us to wait in Jerusalem, in our
> places of mission, until we are renewed by the promise of the
> Father, the Spirit, His power that will come from above . . .
> It is our collective conviction that we Maryknoll Sisters
> should be in El Salvador at this time. It is here that we must
> preach Christ crucified, resurrected and gifting us with God's
> promise.[22]

Due to the hundreds of international press, television, and radio
people who were in San Salvador that day, the news traveled
quickly throughout the world. In New York, Maura watched in
horror as the scene on the cathedral steps flickered across the TV
screen. She read every article in the papers and lived through the
account sent back from El Salvador by the Sisters who were there.
In a very short time she would be ready to return to Nicaragua or
El Salvador. Her constant prayer was that she might be less fearful.

Ita received the news of Archbishop Romero's death while still
in Chile and heard the news of his funeral while in the Panama
airport on her way to Nicaragua. She wrote to her mother:

> I don't even know how to begin this letter, how to react to
> the last week and a half. The Archbishop's death started a
> continental examination of conscience about how each local
> Church was or wasn't being faithful to the Gospel . . . For
> myself, I have all sorts of reactions—from feeling robbed of

not having had the opportunity to know Monseñor Romero, to horror at the paranoia and fear of the right and their brutality, to wonder at the Gospel message and the impact for acceptance or rejection that it has on people, to feeling with the poor of Salvador and their loss of someone whom they knew cared for them. But we believe that his death will bear fruit, and it's part of the Christian mystery we celebrate this week, and in that same Christian tradition, we'll go to El Salvador.[23]

Carla and Sister Madeline Dorsey spent Holy Week in Santa Ana and, on Easter Monday, boarded a bus that took them through Honduras into Nicaragua to meet Ita. "Once over the border into Nicaragua," Maddie remembered, "Carla changed into her T-shirt which was painted with a welcome for Ita who was waiting for us in Leon."[24]

Ita was happy to see Carla, though her apprehensions about the situation into which they were going put a damper on her spirits. Ita wrote to her former roommate Kate Monahan Gregg and her husband:

My timing couldn't be worse, I know, but this is a culmination of a process which began last August when the need was seen to reinforce the group here. Actually, I'm still reeling from Romero's death because we were supposed to work with him and in some way I guess I feel that part of my future was robbed. I appreciate that many people will be concerned about us. We're also concerned for each other and will be doing our best to support and care for each other. It's been a week of free-floating anxiety but I think I'm pretty grounded now and with fear and faith we'll get on the bus tomorrow for El Salvador.[25]

Julie was with Ita and Carla the night before they left. As they prayed together, Carla suggested that Julie let the Bible fall open where it would.

It opened to Psalm 144. There's a line in that psalm that says, "You who give victory to kings and safety to your servant David. . ." It's silly, but once, in the novitiate at Topsfield,

Ita said our friendship was like that of David and Jonathan.
She would sometimes call me "Jon" and every once in a while
would sign a letter "David." From that night on I prayed that
psalm for her.[26]

CHAPTER 13

"Lord of the Impossible"

When Carla and Ita made their decisions to go to El Salvador, they were fully aware of the violence and the confusion in that suffering little country. What neither of them could have anticipated, however, prior to Archbishop Romero's death, was their own confusion and that of the archdiocese as to what they would do there.

In the wake of Romero's murder, the courage, vision, and unity of the Church personnel had deteriorated significantly. Six priests had left the country within several weeks, and those who remained were overworked and largely silent in the face of continuing persecution. Ita and Carla wrote that "the constant violation of human rights by the state and security forces, produces, from our observation, a type of 'state of shock' among the Salvadoran pastoral agents, as well as frustration and impotence caused by the silence of the hierarchical Church."[1]

On April 15 they drew up a one-month plan which, in broad strokes, had two objectives: to become acquainted with the country and the Church of El Salvador and investigate concrete job possibilities.

Ita or Carla, or both of them, were with Maddie in Santa Ana for twenty days of the month, visiting neighbors, participating in prayer groups, burying the dead, listening to stories, becoming acquainted with the people and familiar with their world. Occasionally they would go to the port city of La Libertad where Sisters Teresa Alexander, originally from Yellow Springs, Ohio, and in Central America since 1959, and Joan Petrik, who had previously been in Guatemala, worked in close collaboration with members of a team of missioners from the diocese of Cleveland, Ohio. Untold hours were spent in the hot and dusty buses as they traveled around the country, visiting Church personnel, seeing their works, and asking advice on how they—two new people—might best be able to serve.

They attended national and diocesan meetings of religious, becoming acquainted with all and friends with many, and hoped to spend several weeks with a community of Sisters who worked in the distant country "because neither of us has *campo* experience."[2] In the end, all concerned thought it best to abandon the idea since, as the Cleveland team told them, "The people are so traumatized that they are understandably suspicious and frightened of strangers who all of a sudden appear in their villages saying they want to help."[3]

They visited the area of Soyopango and attended a weekend workshop for sixty rural religious leaders, "all farmers, with an extraordinary faith and simplicity," Ita wrote to her mother. "It was awe-inspiring, listening to them talk of their experience."[4]

"So many of them said, 'I know that commitment to the Lord may mean death,' " Carla wrote, " 'but I believe I will not die forever, but will rise again as Monseñor Romero lives on in our commitment to the truth.' Wow! I really received a lot from them!"[5]

They met with the Vicar-General of the Archdiocese of San Salvador, Monseñor Urioste, and Apostolic Administrator Rivera y Damas. Both men reiterated what Archbishop Romero had told Sister Regina McEvoy, vice president of the Maryknoll Sisters, the year before: the priorities of the Church in El Salvador were relief work with refugees in Cuscatlan, Soyopango, and most especially, in Chalatenango.

Father Cesar Jerez, a native of Guatemala and Superior of the Jesuits in Central America, an approachable man, quick to laugh and full of peace and prayer, also favored Chalatenango. "I know Chalatenango, had been there a number of times," Father Jerez remembered later.

> I very clearly pointed out to them the importance of such a work and how advantageous it would be to be able to do it with a group such as the Assumption Sisters for whom I hold great esteem for their deep Christian values and their commitment to the poor. I admired Carla's and Ita's dedication, their simplicity and commitment, the one rather large like the

strong woman in the Gospel, the other fragile, like a reed in the desert.[6]

As they were leaving Father Jerez's office, Carla asked, "Cesar, what would be the possibility of your giving us spiritual direction?"

"You've got to be kidding!" he answered. "I have no time for directing a couple of pious women who have no need of it." They all laughed and in the end agreed that when they were all in San Salvador and had some unrushed time, they would see each other.[7]

An estimated 200,000 people were living in the roughly 2,000 square kilometers of the department of Chalatenango when Carla and Ita arrived in El Salvador. Sixty percent of the arid mountainous area was planted in small plots of millet and beans by peasants. Historically, Chalatenango had been a conflictive zone due to the peasants' attempts to organize themselves into unions to resist the oppression. As the unions incorporated themselves into the ranks of the popular organizations, repression grew. In May, when the peasants would normally be sowing their crops, the "security forces" were waging operations to "pacify" and "clean out" the area. Many peasants were tortured, mutilated, and killed during raids on villages; others fled to the hills or to other parts of the department; still others, 1,200 by June, had escaped into Honduras.

In a town Carla and Ita had recently visited, twenty-five people were massacred and the security forces would not allow the bodies to be buried. "So the families of the twenty-five people watched them being eaten by vultures," Carla wrote, "and a typhoid epidemic is in full swing."[8]

The level of violence and the depth of suffering were incomprehensible to Carla and Ita. The confusion and apparent paralysis of many people about doing anything to counteract the violence and ease the suffering took its toll in frustration and anger. And yet, they both agreed that "it is good for us to be here."[9] As Ita wrote:

I don't know if it is in spite of, or because of the horror, terror, evil, confusion, lawlessness, but I do know that it is right to be here. To activate our gifts, to use them in this situation, to believe that we are gifted in and for Salvador now, that the answers to the questions will come when they are needed, to walk in faith one day at a time with the Salvadorans along a road filled with obstacles, detours and sometimes washouts—

this seems to be what it means for us to be in El Salvador. It's
a privilege to come to a Church of martyrs and people with a
strong committed faith.[10]

Toward the end of May, Carla and Ita met with the vicar of the
department in Chalatenango, Father Fabian Amaya, and other
Church personnel in order to assess the situation in the vicariate
and see if and how they might be able to help.

Carla and Ita told the assembled priests and Sisters that though
their experience was limited to Chile, principally in an urban
setting with neighborhood groups, they were willing to do whatever
needed to be done. Then they listened as the priests and religious
from different places within the vicariate described the violence
and told of village after village where the people had to flee to the
hills. There were thousands of hungry, sick, and terrified people in
need of food, some sort of refuge, medicines, and the reassurance
that someone cared about them and wanted to help them. In each
of the sixteen parishes of the department, attempts were being
made to deal with immediate daily emergencies, but the scattered
efforts needed to be organized and full-time people had to be
enlisted to coordinate the purchase and delivery of food and medicines, to contact and transport refugees to designated parish houses
and churches. Data on human rights violations needed to be gathered from the "grass roots" and sent to the archdiocesan offices and
the National Commission on Human Rights. Money needed to be
found for beans and transportation and first aid kits. The project
was vast, its importance immeasurable. Ita and Carla decided to
take it on.

"Thank you," Father Amaya spoke for everyone at the meeting.
"If only it were possible for us to end this war," he said, weary of
the need for such work.

"I believe that good will win over evil," Carla was convinced,
"that creativity will win over destruction and that peace will win
over war."[11]

As everyone rose and shook hands to say good-bye and thanks,
Father Sigfredo, who had been silent in a shy way for the entire
meeting, approached Carla and Ita and said in his formal manner
that he was driving into San Salvador and would be honored to have
the pleasure of their company if they were going that way. They
replied that yes, they had planned to return to the city and would

be grateful. "*Su servidor*," Padre Sigfredo said as he gently bowed and turned away to get his things.

A few kilometers outside of town, at a curve in that deserted stretch of road, several military men jumped out of the brush and, with machine guns ready, forced them to stop. "Get out. Hurry up. Hands on the hood."

Carla felt defiant and was tempted to ask them what they thought they were doing, but she was afraid enough to remain quiet. Ita trembled. Father Sigfredo was helpless as the soldiers searched the women over and over again.

After a while they went through the motions of searching the car, looking under the hood and behind the back seats.

"Okay," the apparent leader finally said. "You can go now," and the men returned to the bushes.

Carla mentioned the incident in a letter to Becky Quinn.

> Ita and I were out in Chalatenango where we'll no doubt be working. It's a *campo* area, beautiful scenery and very poor and wild. If you knew how the soldiers search us and treat us you'd worry. But I take it as the power of evil really getting back at the good. When we came back with the priest last week, we were stopped, made to get out of the jeep, hands against the side and really treated rough in words and deeds. About five of them had us at gunpoint and we could easily have been shot right there since the hatred of the Church is so tangible and strong. After about one-half hour of this, we were on our way after Father looked under the hood of the car to see if the boys had planted a bomb there. This week we'll go up to Chalatenango again. Who knows what stories I'll have this time.[12]

In a letter to Mrs. Ford, Carla mentions the trip, though not the incident.

> We have just come back from the poorest part of El Salvador. We saw the beautiful poor people, the dedicated priests, the ruthless repression, the faith of a valiant people, and we got one thousand bites of all species of insects. Needless to say we'll go back for more which is the crazy absurd life we've been chosen for and choose.[13]

Until two rooms and an office could be "disoccupied and conditioned" in the rambling and crumbling old rectory in the town of Chalatenango, Ita and Carla were grateful for the hospitality and company of the Assumption Sisters who lived across the street. For the next several weeks, the three Assumption Sisters slept in one room and reserved the other for Ita and Carla, whose comings and goings were largely unpredictable. In between visits to the different parishes to coordinate the relief work, they would drop in on Maddie at Colonia Lamatapec in Santa Ana as often as possible, and they practically commuted to San Salvador to check on supplies and funding requests and meet with archdiocesan personnel as their work, "The Emergency Committee of the Vicariate of Chalatenango," took shape.

When in San Salvador they always stayed with the Assumption Sisters who ran a high school for young women. Ita wrote to her mother:

> They think we are weird birds, because most religious are very conventual, with an ordered schedule, local superiors and more or less stable in one place. Since we're none of those and are creating a job and mechanisms which can't be fully done from one place, they don't know quite what to make of us but possibly they just think all North Americans are slightly crazy, but they take us in for the love of God and the good of the cause.[14]

In June, the Ecumenical Committee for Humanitarian Aid asked Ita and Carla to petition the United States Church to recognize the existing state of civil war. Until war was declared, international norms of behavior were neither respected nor supervised. "We were involved in getting two guerrillas out of the hospital this afternoon," Carla wrote to the Sisters in Chile. "They were eleven and twelve years old. And in the morning an eight-year-old guerrilla was shot and killed there."[15] Nor could shipments of food and medicines arrive from international agencies until war had been declared. "There are a lot of bizarre things that go on in this country including 'help' from Uncle Sam," Ita wrote to René. "It's pathetic that there's millions for army equipment but nothing for humanitarian help until war is declared. Carla keeps asking, 'How many dead make a war? What's the magic number?' "[16]

In a letter to Sister Melinda Roper, Carla and Ita asked that Maryknoll and other Church personnel:

> Come and see the situation so as to help inform the American public who, as a whole, are ignorant of U.S. policy in El Salvador—and of the real danger of intervention.
>
> Since the death of Romero, the news coverage on Salvador has declined to almost nothing. The Ecumenical Committee fears that decisive action will be taken by our government, under the guise of "stopping the subversives" or "containing communism," and that all of Central America will be involved if this happens. It's a heavy scene, but if we have a preferential option for the poor as well as a commitment for justice as a basis for the coming of the Kingdom, we're going to have to take sides in El Salvador—correction, we have.[17]

Carla wrote to anyone she could think of who might be able to influence groups to petition the Red Cross. She told a friend in Appleton, Wisconsin:

> I never really had much hope in little groups in the States pushing for justice, since I saw the United States government as a monstrous war machine that stepped on little countries with no criteria or control. However, here the people *do* believe in the power of the *pueblo*, the power of the people of the United States to stop a possible U.S. intervention, so I believe with the *pueblo*. I trust that you will do what you can; I ask no more.[18]

Often it seemed that they were spending far more time with papers than with people. The myriad and occasionally unrelated steps in the "Byzantine process" of acquiring their permanent visas took hours of their time and months to complete. Also unending was the correspondence back and forth to international funding agencies. As archdiocesan staff, they received $50 apiece per month for living expenses but were expected to take the responsibility of raising funds for the project. A foundation in Germany, wanting some assurance of local support for the work, asked the amount of their salary.

Ita was stumped by the question. "Hey, Carla, we have to give ourselves a salary. What amount would you consider to be fair and adequate?"

"Well," she thought out loud, "if I were being paid for this I'd want $150,000. In advance!"

Ita laughed and replied, "I think it's kind of low myself."[19]

Often, in order to check on food supplies or search for someone's missing son or mother, Ita and Carla would visit San Roque, the main refugee center in San Salvador. Sister Christine (Cris) Rody, a member of the Cleveland Diocesan Team, which was always generous when called upon to help with transportation, was with Carla as she tried to reunite several families divided between the two big refugee centers in the city.

Carla spoke to a group of peasant women who squatted on a blanket on the floor or sat uncomfortably on the edge. She told the women that their children were safe in another refugee center on the other side of town, that they were fine but too frightened to be moved. If the women wanted to be taken to their children, Carla told them, she and Sister Cris Rody would drive them in a truck that afternoon.

Many of those women had never been more than a few kilometers from their villages until forced to flee weeks or maybe months before. They had been traumatized by the violent uprooting. Only in the past several days, since coming to San Roque, had they begun to feel that there might exist some harbor from the war.

"Are our children really on the other side of town?" they asked among themselves. "What is on the other side of these thick walls?" They trusted Carla—wanted to trust her—but were afraid.

"We waited at that center for more than an hour and a half," Cris remembered. "Carla had a tremendous sense of respect for the needs of the women, treating them not as commodities to be moved around but as people with sensitivities. We waited until the women decided among themselves and then we took them, without incident."[20]

Carla and Ita lived each day with a sense of urgency, their adrenaline rising to meet the constant state of emergency. Though their days were full, it was difficult to give a simple answer to the question "What do you do?" As Carla answered in a letter in mid-July:

This may seem strange to you, but as the repression and

genocide continue, it becomes harder and harder to do pastoral work. So what do I do? I drive people places—like other Sisters who are more and more afraid to stay in the isolated parts of the country areas—I drive *Caritas* food to refugees of which there are 2,000 families in the Department of Chalatenango. I go to meetings where needs are expressed and frustrations aired and in general very little accomplished. I have come to appreciate what Jesus means when he says, "I am the Way." The way here is daily changing as one tries to respond to this genocidal situation. In one parish where there are no longer any priests or Sisters because of the situation, there were forty-two adult catechists—all forty-two have been brutally murdered. No one wants to be a catechist anymore since it usually means your life and yet we try to attend to these remote parts of the country. That's where I drive priests who don't drive. This weekend we go up to Arcatao where the forty-two catechists were killed. We hope to bring food to fifty families there. It's so hard to see the suffering—and harder yet to know that what you do helps so little. I believe in the Lord of the impossible.[21]

Even belief in the "Lord of the impossible," however, did not protect Ita and Carla from mounting anxiety, which they conveyed in a letter to the Sisters in Chile, at Maryknoll, New York, and to their own Panama/Nicaragua/ El Salvador Region (PANISA) in July 1980.

For the last three months we have had no house of which we could say, "This is our home." Because we arrived at a time when the Church was in mourning and struggling to respond to the problems of daily persecution, we find it difficult to find someone with whom to reflect on this experience. We are pastoral workers used to having people whom we can visit, meet with, etc. Now we have no people—we cannot visit because of the times and the very real fear of placing others in danger because of belonging to the Church, which is one of the security forces' biggest enemies. A certain spontaneous support from the Sisters has been present in notes and prayers. However, given the war situation, our reduced numbers and recent illness of one member here, we have felt quite isolated and alone. Control of the mails as well as of the phones makes it difficult to communicate what is happening here, and your letters are not arriving too frequently. We feel the need of more palpable solidarity. Besides lacking our own home, a stable salary, local Church and tangible regional support, and inventing a job daily, neither of us is an emotional or psychological giant in this crazy situation. We realize that a lot of our energies just go into trying to keep walking down this dark road without becoming as dark as the situation.[22]

Having vented their feelings, they felt better and, more reflectively now, they ended with an appreciation for their experience which, in spite of the difficulties, they were disinclined to give up.

We have learned a total dependence and trust in God, a deepening of our commitment and availability, a coming to know the pastoral agents of the local Church and other missioners; an opportunity to know this situation of repression and all its consequences; an exercise in humility and faith; a coming to know one's personal limitations and basic psychological needs; an awareness of ability to adapt to incredible situations.[23]

In conclusion they said that for the moment they would not encourage anyone to join them in Chalatenango, since it was simply too difficult. At the same time, however, they again pleaded for someone to come to be with Maddie in Santa Ana.

They never expected the ripples that were caused by that paper among Maryknoll Sisters in Chile, PANISA, and New York, but were glad that it served to alert people to the needs of El Salvador. For months, it seemed, they had been making some reference in most of their letters to the need for more personnel, or had asked directly, "Why don't you come?" Maddie had written a particularly persuasive letter to Maura Clarke, who was only weeks away from her return to Nicaragua, a letter that did not introduce a new idea to Maura but simply made more concrete what had been haunting her for months.

For almost a year, whenever Maura was at Maryknoll, New York, she had taken part in conversations about the importance of send-

ing more Maryknoll Sisters to El Salvador. She herself believed in
the urgency of the Church's mission there, but it was not until the
summer arrived that she realized how soon she would have to make
a decision. One day she asked a few of the Sisters who had been in
Central America to meet with her to pray and talk and help her
decide. Word spread, and a group of ten Sisters gathered that
evening. She spoke of how much she missed Nicaragua and how
anxious she was to see her many friends there. And yet she was
afraid of going back, afraid of the loneliness that might engulf her
when she realized how far away she had been while her dearest
friends were changed by the war. "How fair would it be," she asked
herself out loud, "to go back to Nicaragua now that victory had been
won when I had no part in the suffering?"[24]

Maura believed in the work of the Church in El Salvador and
considered it a privilege to be able to accompany the people in their
struggle against repression, but she was afraid—afraid that she
would not be able to stand the sight of such suffering, afraid of her
own death.

"I always think people like Maura have everything all sorted out,
that their paths must be very clear," Sister Pat Haggerty recalled,
remembering that night of prayer, "and then Maura, in all of her
simplicity, showed us her doubts and fears and asked us to help her
to decide."[25]

She was afraid for her parents' sake, too—that Mary and John,
now close to 80 years old, could not stand the strain of worry. One
evening after supper, Maura and her father walked along the
boardwalk at Rockaway as the sea gulls cried. As he puffed on his
pipe, they talked. "Maura," he told her, "I hope you won't be going
to El Salvador."

"Pop," she said gently, "now don't you be worrying about where
I go because I'll only be going where the Lord intends."[26] That was
good enough.

During July 4 weekend, when North Americans across the
country were eating hot dogs and watching fireworks to celebrate
their freedom, and as Maura thought of entering El Salvador, a
grisly item cut into the evening news: In the 150° oven of the
Arizona desert, the dehydrated corpses of thirteen Salvadorans
were found. Four of the dead women had pleaded with the "coy-
ote" (the name given to smugglers of human cargo) who escorted
them to strangle them and release them from their unbearable

thirst. He did, and then died. In the midst of the dead were three
staring, hallucinating women. Strewn about them were the contents of the travelers' suitcases: winter clothes, a Bible, a perfume
bottle empty of its contents, which they had fought to consume.
One of the smugglers who managed to survive, it was said, made it
north to a town named "Why" and then disappeared.[27] Maura was
unusually pensive following the news that night.

In Chalatenango, Carla and Ita were told the story by a family
in town. "There was some good news this week for a family here,"
Ita wrote to her mother.

Their daughter survived the Arizona desert and sun. She
must be in pretty fair shape because she was able to speak by
phone to some relatives in California and identify herself. It
was her third attempt to enter the promised land!

We have a standing joke about all the trouble you and we
are going through so that we can stay in a country so many
nationals are leaving. Immigration is going to give us ninety
more days to get all our papers in order. We lost about two
months' time with a runaround from Chile. Now all we
need is the county clerk's certification of Carla's birth
certificate . . . . [28]

CHAPTER 14

"Receive Me, Lord"

Maura arrived in Nicaragua just in time for the first anniversary of the victory over Somoza.

At five A.M., July 19, we joined the people of OPEN, now called Ciudad Sandino, and boarded one of the 35 buses provided to bring us to a meeting place where we would join thousands of others to march to the plaza for the unforgettable celebration. The sight of so many groups marching in from all over Nicaragua and different parts of Latin America was impressive. I even met some young people whom I had had as students in Siuna when they were small children. Standing in the hot sun for hours, traveling many hours on rough roads or getting drenched by a heavy rainfall could not lessen the palpable spirit of joy and pride that was present.

In the one year that has passed since the end of the war there have been some very significant advances. The program of alphabetization in which thousands of young students and teachers have gone to very isolated and difficult areas in order to teach those who never had the opportunity to learn to read and write has been very well organized and is having a lot of success. Parents speak with pride about their fourteen- and fifteen-year-olds not only teaching but helping the farmers with their work and sharing in their family life. There are many Sisters and priests involved in this crusade. Another very notable step has been the provision of work and needed benefits for the poorest class. The effort to raise food production, communal farms, the construction of roads and housing is gradually providing more jobs. The creation of neighborhood grass roots groups in which all have a voice is an effort to have all Nicaraguans participate in the new government.

Since the country was so devastated by the war I expected to find it much worse but the general spirit is one of a new freedom and hope for the future. There are also nice signs like a lovely children's park in the middle of the earthquaked city of Managua, the supermarket once only for the wealthy now filled with the working class and the type of foods they need and the new billboards about the heroes of the revolution as well as town and streets named after them.

I have heard so many stories of suffering, death and heroism from the people of the Christian communities. There are monuments everywhere to each one of the thousands that died in the revolution. In the middle of this mystery of pain there is at the same time such a belief in resurrection—in something new being born.

As well as very noteworthy steps to progress especially for the very poor there are also some problems and doubts. For the most needy, as for everyone, the price of food is very high. Some of the poor do not find things any better as jobs cannot be made available fast enough. Some expected everything to change more rapidly. Some of the businessmen and landowners are dissatisfied because they are feeling taxation for the first time. The fear of counterrevolution is a very real concern for the governing board (junta) as the success of Nicaragua's revolutionary process is not desired by other Latin American rightist and military governments because this little country is serving as a model and a sign of hope for real change for the betterment of the *pueblo* in Latin America. My perception right now is that most Nicaraguans see Fidel Castro as a fellow revolutionary who has encouraged and helped them greatly but is not standing in the way of their developing their own type of government which they believe will not be communistic. What is very hopeful is the role the Church has played and continues to play in being very close to the people in their suffering and struggle.[1]

Though immersed in the "New Nicaragua," Maura was already partly in El Salvador. She read Carla's and Ita's paper and was drawn by their pleas for someone to be with Maddie. And yet, after having heard stories of the war in Nicaragua, she was more afraid than ever of El Salvador. She wrote to her parents:

I would really love to stay here in Nicaragua, but I know I must go to El Salvador to see if it is right for me to be there. Don't worry about me, the Lord takes care of us all. Pray that the work of God in freeing his people here and everywhere in the world can become more evident and grow in strength. We must not be afraid. No matter what happens, we are one with God and with one another.[2]

Several days before Maura's arrival in El Salvador, Ursuline Sister Dorothy Kazel, a member of the Cleveland team in La Libertad, asked Teresa Alexander to come to her house as soon as possible. She had something important to tell her. "She had heard through a very reliable person," Terry remembered, "that the police had been around our house asking many questions about Joan Petrik who had just gone home. She urged me not to sleep there but to move to the apartment above the school."[3] Dorothy was leaving within a few days to visit her family in the United States, and Jean Donovan, a lay missioner with whom she shared the apartment, was grateful for Terry's company.

When Maura arrived on August 5, she helped Jean Donovan and Terry move beds and tables from the house to the back of the church for storage until Carla's and Ita's house in Chalatenango was ready for furniture and habitation.

Maddie, Carla, and Ita came the next day to welcome Maura and meet with Sister Ellen McDonald, who had been asked by the Central Governing Board at Maryknoll to stop to see them on her return to Panama following a visit with her family in Syracuse, New York. When Carla's and Ita's paper was read at Maryknoll, serious concern was expressed for the Sisters in El Salvador.

Maura wrote of her first days in La Libertad:

We had a community meeting all day Thursday. The point kept coming up—you don't have to stay, you should feel free to go. The answers from the four who have been here a little while—one five years and the others only three or four months—was that they believe deeply that God wants them to be here and they don't want to be anywhere else, although why God wants them here is what they are searching out.

The above strangely reflects where I am, I believe. The deep pain or fear hasn't really touched me yet. I hear about

it and have witnessed it somewhat as we saw five dead men
thrown by the roadside on Saturday and one in the town
where we went for Mass yesterday.[4]

She also went with Terry to a meeting with the catechists.
"These are the most rugged, browned, simple and faith-filled men
and women who are religious leaders of their various *pueblos*,"
Maura explained in a letter.

It takes courage for them to continue any celebration of the
Word or meetings because anyone suspected of being in an
organization or attached to the Church is in serious danger. I
was so impressed by this little group that met with Terry
yesterday. The poor really strip you, pull you, challenge you,
evangelize you, show you God . . .[5]

Several days later, Maura and Maddie drove two and one-half
hours to Colonia Lamatapec, Santa Ana, where Maddie had been
alone for months. Lamatapec was a dense collection of 1,200 little
homes built on the site of a former coffee plantation by the residents themselves. Given the chance to move their families from
the inhuman dwellings that were their only choice when they
moved from the countryside to Santa Ana, the people of Lamatapec
worked together on Saturdays to build their homes. It began as a
place of hope, but in those months, with unemployment at 80
percent and political violence on the rise, life was cruel. There were
several deaths from political violence each week.

Maura went with Maddie one evening to a house where the
people were holding a wake for a young man who had been shot by
the security forces the night before—ten minutes before curfew
and a few steps from his own door.

But it was loneliness that afflicted Maura more seriously than
fear. "Dearest friend," she wrote to Kay Kelly, "I wasn't really
feeling loneliness and separation greatly until yesterday when it hit
me. I started this letter to you last night when I felt down in the
depths. . . . "[6]

Though Maura's loneliness lingered for months, she was not
withdrawn or distant. As was true throughout her life, she quickly
came to love the people and they to love her. She wrote to her
parents:

You would see a difference in them from the Nicaraguans, as they are perhaps more down to earth and serious, very hard-working. The children are especially attractive to me. Their dark, almost black eyes are large and dreamy. I visited a poor crippled woman today whose little grandson of seven was cooking, washing the clothes for her and putting wet packs on her swollen leg. He had the loveliest whimsical smile. Surely the Lord must have a plan of hope and happiness for this precious little lad.[7]

As Maura was "getting to know the people" and trying to feel at home, Carla and Ita were finally settling into Chalatenango, "now we finally have a place we can call our own," Carla wrote to Mrs. Ford, "a house within a house."[8]

Their one large room was divided in half, one side serving as kitchen-dining-living area, the other half partitioned to make four small rooms: a bedroom for each, a chapel, and an office. In each plywood cubicle there was just enough space for a bed and a small table that the Cleveland team had delivered from La Libertad. Each also had a tiny closet, more than enough room for the few blouses, slacks, and skirt each owned. They named their house "El Camino Real" after the luxury hotel in San Salvador.

Their spirits were lifting, thanks to the house, but also because of the many letters their Sisters and friends had written since reading the complaint in their report, "your letters are not arriving too frequently." They were concretely aware now of what they never seriously doubted—the Sisters in Chile and Maryknoll, New York, were conscious of the seriousness of the situation and concerned and supportive. Carla wrote to Sister Kathy Gilfeather in Chile:

Thank you very much for your letter and your words from the heart. I read your letter over and over because it was just like being with you. Your words were consoling and, I must admit, it is rather different here from Chile. Civil war is messy, no doubt about that. It's also frustrating when one is of the Church and God who is for people and not for this side or that. At present I am chauffeuring a young priest who has been threatened. I drive food to different places, talk with different people, carry on and on with the Lord about what is happening with this valiant *pueblo.*

The Salvadorans are sharp and strong and have nerves of steel. In one place in the *campo* in the middle of Mass when the shooting started, the women just got up, looked around and knelt down, the men closed the doors, and the priest whom I drive, Sigfredo, just stood and waited and then continued Mass. No hysteria, no leaving the church, just a bit of commotion as Carla sits on the bench and looks around and says inside, "What have I come to?"

It's a barrel of laughs—especially as the priest whom I chauffeur says, "Step on the gas!" over roads that even Toyota ads wouldn't come near to describing. So, the walk continues and the Lord of the Way leads each day with no map and no clear weather, but rather fog and total trust. But after it all—like Peter, I'm glad I jumped out of the boat and said, "If it's you, Lord, bid me come," and He says, "Come." So I dolly on the waves, sinking, screaming out but holding His hand. I know He's here and I'm glad I am. . . .[9]

Ita too was paradoxically at peace. On the occasion of her niece Jennifer Sullivan's birthday, she wrote of the meaning of life she had found in El Salvador.

I want to say something to you, and I wish I were there to talk to you because sometimes letters don't get across all the meaning and feeling. But I'll give it a try anyway.

First of all, I love you and care about you and how you are. I'm sure you know that. And that holds if you're an angel or a goof-off, a genius or a jerk. A lot of that is up to you and what you decide to do with your life.

What I want to say, some of it isn't too jolly birthday talk, but it's real. Yesterday I stood looking down at a sixteen-year-old who had been killed a few hours earlier. I know a lot of kids even younger who are dead. This is a terrible time in El Salvador for youth. A lot of idealism and commitment are getting snuffed out here now.

The reasons why so many people are being killed are quite complicated, yet there are some clear, simple strands. One is that many people have found a meaning to live, to sacrifice, struggle and even die. And whether their life spans sixteen years, sixty or ninety, for them their life has had a purpose. In many ways, they are fortunate people.

Brooklyn is not passing through the drama of El Salvador, but some things hold true wherever one is, and at whatever age. What I'm saying is that I hope you can come to find that which gives life a deep meaning for you, something that energizes you, enthuses you, enables you to keep moving ahead.

I can't tell you what it might be. That's for you to find, to choose, to love. I can just encourage you to start looking and support you in the search.

Maybe this sounds weird and off the wall, and maybe no one else will talk to you like this, but then, too, I'm seeing and living things that others around you aren't. I hope this doesn't sound like some kind of a sermon because I don't mean it that way. Rather, it's something that you learn here and I want to share it with you. In fact, it's my birthday present to you. If it doesn't make sense right at this moment, keep this and read it some time from now. Maybe it will be clearer. Or ask me about it, OK?[10]

At the end of July, Ita and Carla acquired a "secondhand Jeep to roam the back roads of Chalatenango," Ita wrote to her mother. "Carla has baptized it 'La Tonquita' which, roughly translated, means 'Miss Piggy.' It takes to the alleged roads like a pig in a puddle."[11] They could move more quickly now, and freely, without having to depend upon the availability of a parish Jeep or the undependable bus with its fixed and limited routes. On certain occasions, however, they still called upon the Cleveland team to help them out.

Reports had been received of 3,000 people hiding in the mountains, waiting for a promised "final offensive" by the peasants organized against the security forces who caused them to flee. As the days stretched out and hunger increased and sickness spread, a message was sent to Chalatenango saying that 200 women, children, and old people wanted to go into San Salvador to the refugee center.

Ita contacted the Red Cross to arrange for a bus to be sent to a certain rendezvous point for them at 9:30 one Saturday morning.

Meanwhile, Carla met a priest who had thirty children in his parish house and wanted them moved to the city. Cris Rody remembered:

> So Carla got in touch with Jean Donovan and me and asked if we could go up with our truck to take the children to the rendezvous point. We went and picked up the children and were on our way when two troop carriers made us stop. We thought it was curtains for everyone but the commander just wanted to ask the priest if he would give refuge to some rightist refugees. It's a very confusing situation. The rightists had the roads blocked off so no one could come down out of the hills that day. The only ones moved to the city were the thirty children.[12]

Many people expressed concern for Carla and Ita's safety as they traveled through the hills. They too were well aware of the dangers. Carla wrote to Mrs. Ford:

> We've been transporting refugees and "hot" priests to different country areas, but I believe the Lord protects us and no harm will come to us. This is a unique experience and I admit I do try to protect Ita although she doesn't like that. As far as risk goes, I never invite her to accompany me in a risky thing. In this insane situation who's to know what is risky and actually all we're doing is very humanitarian.
>
> There is a certain amount of freedom for me since contact with my family is so minimal. I always say to Ita that if anything happens to me, she has only to advise Maryknoll, but should she be harmed, I dread having to advise the Ford Foundation.
>
> The time of the crunch could be getting closer and communication may be difficult or impossible. Please know that we trust in the Lord of Life and I expect you to do the same.[13]

Though the increasing demands of their work prevented them from having a weekly day of fasting and prayer as they would have wished, each "escaped" to the Assumption convent in San Salvador or to Santa Ana as often as she could. On Thursday morning, August 21, Carla was preparing to drive into San Salvador for the first such day in many weeks. Before she left they had read the Scripture, "I will take away your hearts of stone and give you hearts of flesh."

"God has already done that for me," Carla told Ita, and then told her of the time, years before in Chile, when she had prayed for a heart of stone.

"I've come miles since then, and you've walked a lot of that road with me," she continued. Then she prayed, "Now you can dismiss your servant in peace, O Lord."

"I'm not so sure I get dismissed so easily," Ita had misunderstood.

"We'll see," is all Carla said.[14]

In San Salvador, Carla prayed the Divine Office with the Sisters and then walked to the cathedral to sit in front of Archbishop Romero's unadorned tomb to pray. There were flowers and pieces of paper pasted everywhere with penciled messages, "*Gracias, Monseñor*," or "Pray for us."

On Friday Carla spoke to Sister Ana Graciela's senior high school students at the Assumption Sisters' Colegio de la Asuncion about the missionary vocation, of the many people who needed help and the inherent danger of being charitable without at the same time working for justice. They were left pensive by her use of a quote from St. Vincent de Paul: "We should apologize to the poor for our charity towards them," for those young women were daughters of the not so poor.

Before driving back to Chalatenango that afternoon, Carla picked up the mail and a shipment of medicines at the Chancery Office. She took the pills out of the bottles and wrapped them in plastic bags that she hid under the seats and in the darker corners of the Jeep, hoping they would not be confiscated at the military roadblocks along the way. She was home before dark in time for a supper of rice and beans that they and the in-transit refugees shared from a common pot.

The next day, Saturday, August 23, Carla left early to drive Padre Sigfredo to a number of *campo* places for Mass and to deliver food and first aid kits Ita had assembled the day before. "It's a schizophrenic thing that such supplies are considered 'war materials' by those who seem reluctant to admit that this is, in fact, a war,"[15] Ita said. Irrational or not, the first aid kits were considered subversive by the security forces, and Carla tried to make them inconspicuous.

Ita stayed in town that day to check on some missing persons whose names had been given her the day before. "It's kind of urgent," Ita explained, "that someone make a fuss about missing persons as soon as possible so that not only are the proper people aware of the fact that someone's disappearance is known, but also that they will think twice about their completely disappearing."

Ita went to the army base shortly after Carla drove out of town to present the list to the colonel, "an eccentric man," Ita called him, "a man who labeled the Church 'subversive' because it's on the side of the weak." Occasionally the colonel would release a prisoner to Church personnel, "perhaps to save face," was Ita's theory, and he released one to her now.

It was late afternoon when she returned with him to the parish center where about five refugee families were housed temporarily, "people whose husbands and sons had been killed the week before in San Antonio de Los Ranchos."

"Madre," one of the women whispered to Ita as the recently freed prisoner, a man who had betrayed some leftist neighbors to the security forces, settled himself into a corner of the large room, "we know that man and cannot trust him. If he recognizes us he will tell those who killed our husbands and sons that we are here."

Ita managed to distract the young man until, greatly relieved and tired of conversation, she heard the Jeep pull up outside. Though it would soon be dark and rain was imminent, Carla and Ita decided that the only thing to do was to take the man to his home about thirty minutes away. They asked Esteban and Alfredo, the two seminarians who lived in the parish center, to go along with them.

"We were just about ten minutes outside of Chalatenango when one of those really freaky, heavy rains began," Ita recalled. "We had the choice of two roads. One has no rivers along it but it had a lot of landslides (and we thought) the other was the better way to go, the one where you cross the same El Chapote River about five times."

They had crossed four of the bends, but at the edge of the fifth, beyond which was the prisoner's town, Carla announced emphatically, "I'm not going through that. It looks kind of ugly, and I'm not sure I can cross that."

"Okay, out you go," Ita told their passenger.

"It looks like it's going to be hard for me to cross that," he complained.

"Here's the story." Ita was impatient and anxious to return to the other side of those streams. "We're not going to stay here and we're not going to cross that river. We are going back to Chalatenango. If you want to stay here, you stay." He finally reluctantly got out and watched as Carla turned the Jeep around and went back to recross the stream they had crossed not more than five minutes earlier. Suddenly it was raging, wide, and three to four feet deep. The Jeep was being dragged into the torrent.

"The land is over there!" Ita pointed to the road by which they had come.

"We are being taken," Carla replied steadily but with helplessness in her voice.

"We are going to die! We are going to drown!" One of the two young men was frantic.

"No, we're not going to die." Ita tried to resist the terror. "Let's just see what happens."

The two young men scrambled out and attempted to pull Ita and Carla against the onrushing water.

"Come on, get out." The two men had Ita's arms.

"Just then," Ita remembered, "the Jeep turned over and the driver's side went down, the door closed, and the river started to come in." At that, Carla pushed Ita through the window.

"I went bobbing down the river and I couldn't believe it was so far down. I went down very deep and I said to myself, 'You're not going to get up,' so I said, 'Receive me, Lord.' "

Three kilometers downstream, after an interminable time spent tossing and turning and being thrown against the rocky bottom of the stream, Ita grabbed hold of some roots where she clung until "in a voice which seemed to be other than my own I said, 'The Lord has saved you to continue serving the poor and you've got to get out of this river.' "

She tried again and again to force her aching body up the high, slippery bank. "Thirty or forty tries" and an hour later she managed to pull herself up and stumbled through the darkness, tripping through beans and knocking down stalks of corn, to curl up under a wild bush. For the rest of the night she trembled from exhaustion and the cold, unable to rouse enough strength to swat at the swarms of mosquitoes that bit her all night long. At some point she did hear a distant cry, "We're looking for the madres, we're looking for the madres," but she could not move.

"While I was up there I had no idea of what happened to Carla or to Esteban or Alfredo," Ita recalled. "I had to think that they could be alive or they could be dead."

At six the next morning the announcement came again. "We're looking for the madres."

"Well," Ita went on, "I got myself up and started making my way down the mountain. When I got down to the river bank I started to call and some man came along and I said, 'Did you hear what they are saying? I'm one of those people.' So he crossed the river and took me home to his house and gave me a towel to put around me and we started to walk towards town."

Along the way, in a little settlement, some women gave Ita a set of dry clothes and tended to her cuts with a first aid kit that Ita had assembled on Friday and Carla had delivered less than twenty-four hours earlier.

Maddie, Maura, and Terry left Santa Ana and La Libertad early that morning, as soon as they received an alarming and garbled message about an accident in Chalatenango, and found Ita with the doctor when they arrived. She was bruised, scratched, covered with innumerable mosquito bites, and "hyper" in her exhaustion. Still feeling cold, she asked for a cup of hot coffee while the search for Carla continued through the long morning. It seemed the whole town was involved in the search, and people were in and out of the Sisters' house checking on Ita and on the progress of the search parties. Finally, close to noon, the Red Cross found her. Her broken, twisted, naked body had been washed up on a sand bar in the now tame river, fourteen kilometers from where the Jeep had foundered the night before.

CHAPTER 15

Carla's Grave

They carried Carla to the little house-within-a-house, wrapped her in a blanket, and laid her on the bed. As people from the town came in—curious, somber, grieved—they lifted the blanket to look at her face.

The archdiocese sent the longest ready-made coffin they could find. "Not too many people 5'8" around," Ita explained. "They had to bury her without shoes, but in her rainbow dress."[1]

Bishop Rivera y Damas went from San Salvador for a Mass that afternoon, and the Assumption Sisters' chapel in the city was offered for the wake, "but I said no," Ita continued. "She died right here working for these people. She belonged to them and they belonged to her and this is not the time to march her off."

The Sisters kept urging Ita to return to bed. She was exhausted and her lungs were affected by her large intake of river water. But Ita could not give in. For one thing, she wanted to choose the Scripture readings for the funeral liturgy. "I wanted the one from Romans, 'Nothing can separate you from the love of God.' And the Gospel that says, 'There is no greater love than to lay down your life for your friends.' I think Carla died doing what she wanted to do."

The wake lasted throughout the night, the people coming and going, praying and singing, sitting in silence and half-sleep. The Assumption Sisters, the Cleveland team, Maddie, Maura, Terry, slept in snatches on cots or on the floor. At the funeral Mass the next morning, the church was full. Ita reported:

Some refugees came who were supposed to be on death lists and were in hiding. They came in, paid their respects and quietly left again.

Then we went to the cemetery. It is down two streets and

then down a big long hill which leads to the entrance to the town and it was muddy and slippery. All of the Sisters who were there wheeled the coffin down and I was holding on behind. It occurred to me that this would be the last time I'd ever have to try to hold Carla back.

Carla and I had talked lots of times about the possibility of our dying because of things here, very violent things. We talked about how difficult it would be if we weren't together for the one who was left behind. At the very end of St. John's Gospel there is a little scene of Jesus with Peter, and John seems to be in the background. Jesus says to Peter, "Follow me." Peter turns around and says, "What about him?" And Jesus says, "I'm telling you to follow me and he's to wait until I return." If John was within hearing distance, how did he feel? I think we know now.

Julie Miller flew from New York to San Salvador on Monday with Sister Peg Hanlon, a native of San Francisco who, after several years in mission in Bolivia, had been elected to the Central Governing Board at Maryknoll. Julie stayed for several days with Ita as she rested in the hospital.

Father Cesar Jerez was one of Ita's many visitors during the week and recalled that, though Ita was angry and hurt that God would have permitted such a thing, there was, even then, a hint of playfulness in her. "Cesar," she whispered conspiratorially, "they will listen to you. Tell them not to take me out of here. I want to stay in El Salvador."[2]

"I laughed with her," Father Jerez recalled, "and said that though I don't have any high influence in Maryknoll I would do what I could. Very discreetly, then, I spoke to Sister Peg Hanlon."[3]

While waiting for Ita to be released from the hospital, Peg met with Father Amaya, Father Urioste, the vicar of the archdiocese, and the Chancellor, Father Urrutia. All of them said that though they would understand if the Maryknoll Sisters decided to leave El Salvador, they nonetheless reiterated their hope that more Sisters would come.

The next day Peg spoke with Bishop Rivera y Damas about Sister Joan Petrik's possible return. "During the meeting," Peg remembered, "we received word that a seminarian had been picked up, tortured with electric shocks on the legs and, among other things, had been asked where Joan Petrik was. That seemed to convince everyone that she should not go back."[4]

Dorothy Kazel returned from a visit to the United States the day Ita was released from the hospital and brought the long-awaited copy of Carla's birth certificate, the last paper needed to complete the process for her resident visa.

On Sunday, one week after Carla's body had been found, the Sisters went to a little hotel by the beach to spend a few days together planning for the future. Dorothy and Jean Donovan packed peanut butter, cheese, and crackers and insisted that they take the white van for as long as they might need it.

Once everyone saw how determined Ita was to remain not only in El Salvador but in the work she and Carla had begun in Chalatenango, Maura said that though she was afraid of the dangers and aware of the fact that she could never take Carla's place, she would love to return with Ita. Relieved and grateful, Ita told Maura that her gentleness and compassion were the greatest gifts anyone could give to the terrified refugees and to her.

It was decided that rather than leave Maddie alone again, Terry would turn over her work with the catechists in Taminique to the Cleveland team and move to Santa Ana.

The night before Peg and Julie returned to New York, as they were praying with Ita, Julie reminded her of the night before she and Carla left Nicaragua for El Salvador. "Do you remember the psalm we prayed?"

"Yes," Ita replied, "I remember it mentioned David and Jonathan."

"I have prayed that psalm for you every day since then," Julie told her, "but not until after Carla's death did I notice the line, 'Save me, rescue me from the deep waters.' Now, according to the psalm, all you have to worry about is 'the power of aliens.' "

"Julie, do me a favor." Ita smiled. "Don't stop praying it now."[5]

Maura returned to Santa Ana with Maddie until Terry could make arrangements with Dorothy and Jean and the catechists for her work to continue. Ita, after two weeks of constant company, night and day, simply wanted to be alone. Terry was reluctant to leave her but gave in when Ita assured her that she would be fine at the Assumption Convent and welcomed having a few errands to do, such as going to the immigration office to get permission to leave the country for a scheduled retreat in Guatemala and delivering Carla's death certificate to the American Embassy.

Later that afternoon, Terry was still en route to La Libertad from San Salvador when Ita called. She was crying. Jean Donovan answered the phone and listened as Ita told of her trip to the American Embassy. When she went to leave Carla's death certificate, the official pointed out to her that not only was Carla's name misspelled but that the judge's certification of death was inadequate because it did not mention in what volume and on what page her death was noted. "Who could ever prove that she is dead?" the woman asked.

"I offered to sign another statement that I personally saw her buried," Ita wrote to her mother, "but they said I would have to return to Chalatenango to get official papers with all of the seals."[6] It was then that Ita finally broke down.

She stayed several weeks with the Assumption Sisters, "praying, thinking, strolling around the corners of the garden where she and Carla used to pray,"[7] Sister Ana Graciela recalled. Ita made a tape for her mother and wrote letters in which she shared her search to understand.

> This is kind of a heavy experience, but I guess it just says that God is extremely active in our lives and is certainly the Lord of life, the one who's in charge, the one who decides. I've come in contact with a lot of people who sleep outside at night. They say they sleep in the hills. These are the things that bind you to people. I'm sure that what all this means will come about and be clearer later on. Meanwhile, I must stand humbly before the wisdom and love of our God who chose to call Carla to Himself that night and not me. Our years together are a great gift and source of strength. I miss Carla very much, yet I also believe that we are still bound in a relationship whose depths I still must discover. I believe she is still fully alive and I rejoice with her. May she help us continue serving those whom the Lord puts in our lives.[8]

Ita's faith was strong, but so was the pain, which was all the more intense because her closest friends and Carla's were miles away. Ita wrote to the Sisters in Chile:

> Dear, dear friends, I just had an insight. When someone dies

we all get together to cry, tell stories, laugh, reminisce, pray, have a liturgy and celebrate the fullness of life. And I know you all did that—so many of you who had known and loved Carla longer than I. What hit me was that there is no one in this country who knows Carla for longer than four months. Already she's a little bit larger than life, a heroine, an "angel of charity," and I guess it's useless for me to protest that my beat up ole friend is an example of God's strength being manifest in our weakness; His goodness and love through our vessels of clay.

It's one of those mysteries to be asked to mourn alone when everyone else with whom Carla shared her life is in Chile, New York, even Bangladesh. Next week we'll be going to Guatemala to join the Sisters there on retreat. I think that's a good idea. After that, Maura Clarke and I will go back to Chalatenango. Maura's great gift of kindness and love will be great for the traumatized, hurting people there. She'll be great for me, too.[9]

Before leaving for Guatemala, Maura and Ita made the trip from San Salvador to Chalatenango to assure the people that they would not be gone for more than a few days.

The retreat was a time for the Sisters in Guatemala and El Salvador to look at the situations in which they lived and, through prayer and Scripture, to allow some meaning to emerge, or at least help them grow in trust of the incomprehensible. "The retreat was very serious," Maura wrote to her parents, "but very needed for the time we are living. . . . "[10]

Ita was somber and alone for most of the week and torn by the arrival of what should have been good news. Her good friend Sister Carolyn Lehmann wrote from New York to say she would be stopping in Guatemala to see her on her return to Chile and asked Ita to wait there. The delay, Ita thought, would mean backing down on the promise she had made to the people in Chalatenango that she and Maura would return in ten days. But Maura encouraged Ita to stay and promised to explain why she would be a few days late. Until Ita returned, Maura would stay with the Assumption Sisters across the street.

Carolyn and Ita spent most of that last week of September remembering their years with Carla in Chile. They left the house seldom, once to visit the Sisters on the other side of Guatemala City and another time to buy Ita a gift in the market on what would have been Carla's forty-first birthday.

"Ita and I left Guatemala together," Carolyn recalled, "she getting off the plane in San Salvador and I continuing on to Santiago. I turned to Ita on the plane and said, 'When will we ever see each other again?' She looked at me, shrugged her shoulders and didn't answer. We embraced, said that we loved each other and then Ita left the plane."[11]

In Chalatenango, Ita's and Maura's busy lives resumed. "Being busy is fine for me now—especially on some days when I just don't feel like myself. I guess it's the blahs that come after someone close to you dies. I presume it will pass with time, and in the meantime I'm running Maura ragged."[12]

Maura was sensitive to Ita's grief and tried to protect her from the constant atmosphere of death. If Ita would do the all-important paperwork for the project, Maura suggested, then she would be with the refugees, listening to their horror stories and absorbing their sadness.

Ita telegraphed agencies ("unfortunately telephone numbers are in a book at the bottom of a river"[13]) in order to inquire about archdiocesan funds that should have been deposited. She wrote to Peg Hanlon in New York to ask about the possibility of helping to replace "La Tonquita, which is still parked in Chalatenango, so I have my reality therapy daily."[14] And it was Ita who received the urgent requests for food, medicines, and transportation and was the one who purchased supplies.

"These days I feel like a Chicago merchant," she wrote to Sister Gertrude Vaccaro, another member of the Central Governing Board at Maryknoll, "specializing in grain futures—or maybe Joseph in Egypt—storing grains against the coming shortage. There's nothing more absurd than two Brooklynites judging the quality of red beans and corn!"[15]

There were constant trips into the countryside to deliver supplies or pick up refugees. More often than not, Ita and Maura went along on these trips because the visibility of "gringo" women, particularly if they happened to be citizens of the United States, was considered a guarantee for safety to the driver and refugees.

As before, their friends Dorothy Kazel and Jean Donovan and other members of the Cleveland team were always ready to help.

"Their biggest asset is being blonde," Ita wrote to her mother, "which makes roadblock passing easier. Carla kept threatening to bleach her hair when she saw how they got through."[16]

One day they were called to the parish house in the environs of a town named Adeleita, where sixty people had taken refuge. After unloading the sacks of grain, the women and the old men told their story. For eight months they had had to sleep in the hills in the rain and cold, in fear of night visits from the government-sponsored death squads or the early morning army invasions. They would dare to go down to their homes only in the daylight and with a neighbor on guard so as not to be caught by the security forces. Just the day before, a patrol raided their village, leaving word that the next time they were going to finish off the women and children. That night all the people abandoned the area for good and trekked five hours through the night, guided by the sons and husbands who were defending the area, until they finally reached the parish house at dawn. One woman gave birth to twins an hour after their arrival.

Often during their trips to campo towns, they would come upon bloated bodies on the side of the road. Maura wrote:

> The way innocent people, families, children are cut up with machetes and blessed temples of the Lord thrown and left for the buzzards to feed on them seems unbelievable but it happens every day. The other day passing a small lake in the jeep I saw a buzzard standing on top of a floating body. We did nothing but pray and feel. We don't know how long this can continue but the pain goes on and there are many hungry people hiding and struggling. Being here with Ita and working for the refugees has its sweetness, consolation, special grace and is certainly a gift. The courage and suffering of these people never ceases to call me.[17]

On November 2, the feast of All Souls, the day on which families visit and decorate the graves of their deceased, Maddie, Terry, and Jean Donovan went to Chalatenango to visit Carla's grave.

"The Christian community of Chalatenango must have thought we were very slow in moving," Ita wrote to Peg Hanlon, "so they took it upon themselves to have a marker made for Carla's tomb. It's quite elaborate."[18]

Maura had gone with Padre Sigfredo to celebrate Mass in several communities, but Ita was home with Maddie, Terry, and Jean Donovan when a woman came, quite distraught, to ask for someone's company. "Madre," she spoke to Ita, "a man just came to tell me he thinks he knows where my son is buried. Will you come with me?"

Jean went with Ita and the mother to a little plot of land outside town. A kind farmer was digging. Several minutes later he reached down into the grave to remove a handkerchief he had placed on the boy's face when he buried him two days before.

"That is my son," the mother cried. "Now I can rest, for I know he is at peace and with God."[19]

Ita trembled and tried to remove that sight from her memory.

In spite of the unrelenting violence and their own fears, Maura and Ita were increasingly convinced that they were where they should be and at peace with what they were doing. "We keep plugging along here," Ita wrote to a friend, "because life is threatened by other evils worse than death—hatred, manipulation, vengeance, selfishness."[20] Once again they were asking that other Sisters join them.

The annual regional assembly of Maryknoll Sisters from Panama, Nicaragua, and El Salvador was to be held in Managua within a few weeks. In preparation, Ita and Maura discussed with archdiocesan personnel the pros and cons of inviting more Sisters at that time. The clear direction they received was that "Yes, there is an over-abundance of work due to the evolving war situation. Maryknoll Sisters because of formation, flexibility of life-style and experience in similar situations are seen as very appropriate and needed collaborators in this historical moment."[21]

In San Salvador they spoke with their friend, Father Cesar Jerez. "We spoke for a long time about their work," Father Jerez recalled, "if it was convenient and wise to continue. One of the points we discussed with such simplicity was whether those who come would be willing to die."[22]

Several weeks earlier the Assumption Sisters in Chalatenango had abandoned their convent across the street from the parish house and were sleeping in crowded quarters with Maura and Ita. With violence and retaliation mounting in the area, the Sisters were afraid that the police station, with which their convent shared a wall, might be bombed, and they with it. Ita and Maura mentioned in their letters home that the Sisters were with them at night, though they never said why. Nor did they alarm their families by telling of the death threat that had been posted on their door. "Everyone working here is a communist," it read, "and anyone entering here will be killed."[23] When Padre Efrain Lopez found the note and took it to the comandante of the garrison, he was assured that it must be a prank, "the work of crazy men."[24] The note was not surprising to Ita and Maura—no more ominous than the ever-present threat of death all around them—it was only an unnecessary reminder.

During the third week of November, Ita went to San Salvador to get their visas to leave the country for the regional assembly in Nicaragua. "It's at least a three-day process," Ita wrote. "It's like getting temporary parole from prison—the control is fantastic. And of course no one thinks of scheduling meetings in non-conflictive areas like the Virgin Islands!"[25] Finally, with visas in hand, she arranged for their flight to Managua and then returned to Chalatenango.

Maddie sent a telegram the next day from Santa Ana to Chalatenango, telling Maura and Ita of the plans she and Terry had made and suggesting they try to fly back together on December 2 on the 2:00 P.M. LANICA flight. Ita and Maura's tickets were for a later COPA flight, and it was simply too much trouble to change them. True, it would be more convenient for Dorothy and Jean to make only one trip to the airport that day, but the time and expense involved hardly made it seem worthwhile. They left their tickets the way they were and flew from San Salvador to Managua on the morning of November 24.

CHAPTER 16

Flying Home

The Sisters from Ciudad Sandino were there to greet the flight as it landed at 10:00 A.M. on November 24, and Maura went home with them while Ita continued on to Leon to be with Julie for a day or two.

On November 26, at Diriamba Retreat House outside of Managua, twenty-two Maryknoll Sisters from Panama, Nicaragua, and El Salvador, with guests from Guatemala, Mexico, and the United States, launched their annual regional assembly with a Thanksgiving dinner.

Maura was in good spirits, "at home with the old gang again," but Ita was withdrawn and distracted, unable to enter into the festivities. "I really don't feel very thankful," she told Maryknoll Sister Maria Rieckelman, a psychiatrist from the United States. She talked to Maria of Carla's death and the situation in El Salvador and how hard it was to be constantly among people who were burying their dead or looking for missing family members. She spoke of going to an open grave with a mother to look for her son and said, "I could not do that again."[1]

They spoke of the possibility of Ita's returning to Chile to do her grieving with her friends there, or to the States for awhile. "I'll think about it," she told Maria.[2]

"Maura had arrived in better shape than Ita," Maria recalled,

principally because she was not grieving as heavily for Carla, but also because — though she could not understand it herself — she was dealing with the horror quite well. She spoke of the mutilated bodies and the little children but it was as if she were walking through it with the sense that God was going to bring good out of that tremendous evil, and she was very conscious of her faith.[3]

During Thanksgiving dinner, word was received of the murder of the six members of the executive committee of the Democratic Revolutionary Front in San Salvador.

Ita sincerely tried to be interested and to participate during the first day of meetings, but a terrible inertia seemed to hold her back. On the second day, during a liturgy prepared in memory of Carla and Sister Alice Morrison who, after many years in mission in Central America, had recently died of cancer at Maryknoll, New York, Ita realized for the first time that she was with women who shared her mourning. "She cried quite a bit," Maria remembered, "and from then on she was able to smile and to sleep a bit better and to take part in the meetings, especially the session concerning personnel for El Salvador."[4]

Ita encouraged the group to look for creative and effective ways of inviting Sisters to go to El Salvador. She pointed out that the personnel of the Archdiocese of San Salvador had recovered from the murder of Archbishop Romero and were again strong in their denunciations of the violence and their support for the oppressed, and convinced of the right of the people to determine their own future and form of government. Because of the archdiocesan stand, Ita explained, the Church

is encountering a notable increase in hostility and in incidents that indicate a premeditated persecution. From January through October 1980, there have been twenty-eight assassinations of Church personnel, three woundings, twenty-one arrests, four profanations of the Eucharist, forty-one machine-gunnings of Church buildings, fourteen bombs, and thirty-three search and seizures of Church properties.[5]

Unanimously reaffirming their commitment to support the Church of El Salvador, the Sisters appointed Julie Miller to draft another letter calling for personnel for El Salvador and approved the suggestion that Ita, at a later date, be their traveling spokesperson to Mexico, Guatemala, and South America.

On the last day of meetings, Monday, December 1, Ita told Maria that she didn't think she needed to go to Chile or the United States. "I want to go back to El Salvador," she said, and she smiled to erase any lingering doubts.[6]

That evening they closed the meeting in prayer. Maura acknowledged her fear of the violence and the sight of untold suffering but said she wanted to go back to El Salvador. She felt strong "not in myself but in the sense that the Lord will be faithful to me and his great love will take care of it."[7]

As Maddie read the prayer from the Divine Office of the day, Ita listened intently. "The waves of death rose about me, the torrents of destruction assailed me. The snares of the grave entangled me. The traps of death confronted me. For the poor who are oppressed and the needy who groan, I myself will arise, says the Lord."

"Maddie," Ita later asked her, "where in the world did you find that prayer? Nothing ever grabbed me so much as that."[8]

Ita had also been asked to read, and she chose an excerpt from one of Archbishop Romero's homilies. "Christ invites us not to fear persecution because, believe me, brothers and sisters, one who is committed to the poor must risk the same fate as the poor. And in El Salvador we know what the fate of the poor signifies: to disappear, to be tortured, to be captive and to be found dead."[9]

During the party everyone was full of fun, relieved to have accomplished a great deal in only a few days, and happy to be together, not knowing when the next time might be. Ita seemed to be the most buoyant of all, perhaps because of the contrast to the state in which she had arrived. She surprised everyone by volunteering to be in one of the skits and later jumped up to teach the "barnyard shuffle" as the group sang "Old MacDonald Had a Farm." Maura danced the Irish jig for the last of at least a thousand times.

When the party began to break up later in the evening, some Sisters lingered for awhile and others went to pack or write some last-minute notes to send with Maria to the United States. Maura was one of the few up at dawn to say good-bye to Maria as she left to catch her flight to Miami with an intermediate stop in San Salvador.

"When we landed in San Salvador," Maria remembered, "the flight attendant announced that we would be there only a very short time."[10] Minutes later, three military personnel boarded the plane and studied the passengers from their position at the front of the plane. One of them spoke to the stewardess, who then walked back to question each of the eight remaining passengers. "Where are you going?" she asked when she reached Maria's seat.

"To Miami," she answered.

The stewardess returned to the military men and apparently delivered the eight answers. Again she went to Maria and asked, "Where are you going?"

"I said I was going to Miami," Maria recalled days later. "There were no other North Americans aboard that plane. I am sure there were not."

For the duration of the flight, Maria was ill. When she asked for air sickness bags, the flight attendants seemed afraid to have anything to do with her. In Miami, when she asked for assistance in getting off the plane, she was left alone on board until the cleaning crew found her sometime later. "I don't know whether those women had any notion of what was really going on," Maria pondered later. "They might have been nervous with me as a passenger or they might have been tense because of the whole situation in El Salvador. I don't know."

Back in Managua, after lunch with the Sisters at McDonald's, Maddie and Terry said good-bye and told Maura and Ita that they would ask Dorothy and Jean to pick them up at six o'clock. "Stay with them tonight," Maddie advised them. "No telling what might be going on in the city with the funerals of the Frente leaders tomorrow."[11]

In Ciudad Sandino, while Maura visited with the many friends who had heard she might be there for an hour or two, Ita rested quietly and read.

In San Salvador, the LANICA flight landed at four o'clock and Dorothy and Jean were there with the white van to pick up Maddie and Terry. During the thirty-minute ride to La Libertad, where they would pick up their Jeep, Maddie and Terry told Jean and Dorothy about the meetings and listened to the news of the six murders and the delightful evening the Cleveland team had spent with Ambassador and Mrs. Robert White the night before. As they drove, someone remarked on the unusual absence of military patrols along the highway.

Though it would not be known for weeks, a message was at that moment being dispatched from one military unit to another in the area of the airport. It contained the sentence, "No, she's not on this flight. We'll wait for the next one."[12]

In Managua, around four o'clock, about the time Maddie and Terry's flight arrived in San Salvador, Maura and Ita arrived at the airport to discover that the COPA flight on which they had reservations would be an hour late. Maura and Bea Zaragoza wandered from shop to shop looking for a Christmas gift for Ita. Maura was considering the brightly woven blouse Bea had found. "It can't be too fancy, or she will never wear it."[13]

Bea turned to what was really on her mind. "Maura, do you think you'll ever come back to Nica?"

Maura paused and looked at her friend. "Bea, I really don't think so. I think God wants me in El Salvador."[14]

Julie and Ita also drifted in and out of the stores, not shopping as much as filling the time until good-byes had to be said. "For some reason I bought Ita a cross made of stone," Julie remembered. "It was odd. We usually gave one another gifts only for occasions."[15]

In Chalatenango, the sacristan was discreetly called aside in the movie theater by a member of ORDEN and shown a death list bearing his own name as well as the names of the parish driver, the cook, Padre Efraim Lopez, the Assumption Sisters, Maura, and Ita.

Padre Lopez received a letter accusing all Church workers of being communists, of stirring up trouble and turning people against the government. "Indeed the killings will begin today," it read.[16]

At the airport in Managua, it was suddenly time for the passengers to move through customs and say good-bye. Nothing was said except what was always said, though everyone ached to express more. "Have a good trip. See you soon."

Even after the last few commonplace words, they were not gone but visible, just beyond reach and hearing on the other side of the glass doors, going through the predictably slow emigration process. They turned from time to time to wave, to say they knew their friends were there, to smile, to say good-bye again. One of the Sisters threw up her hands in mock exasperation as if to say, "What's taking so long?" They passed through customs. Ita did a step or two of the "barn yard shuffle" and Maura laughed. Then they were gone.

November 1984

Due to extensive media coverage of the murders of Maura Clarke, Jean Donovan, Ita Ford, and Dorothy Kazel, and the subsequent public outcry in the United States, economic and military aid to El Salvador was temporarily suspended by President Jimmy Carter on December 5, 1980. When the United States Presidential Mission (the Rogers-Bowdler Mission), sent to El Salvador in mid-December, led to the establishment of a Special Investigative Commission by the government of El Salvador, military and economic aid was resumed. On January 21, 1981, however, U.S. Ambassador Robert White informed the State Department that "all the evidence we have . . . is that the Salvadoran government has made no serious effort to investigate the killings of the murdered women." The Tyler Report presented to Congress in December 1983 went even further, concluding: ". . . the identities of the killers were known to officials of the Salvadoran National Guard within days of the murders . . . the initial Salvadoran government response appears to have been to do everything possible to conceal the perpetrators of the crime."

Judge Tyler also suggested that it was "quite possible that Colonel Carlos Eugenio Vides Casanova, then head of the National Guard and now a general and Minister of Defense, was aware of, and for a time acquiesced in, the cover-up."

In spite of the cover-up, continued international public pressure resulted in the arrest of six members of the Salvadoran National Guard on May 9, 1981. Little if anything was done, however, for the next seven months, until the U.S. Congress passed legislation in December 1981 requiring presidential certification of human rights improvements in El Salvador as a condition for further military aid. The provisions of the presidential certification included progress in the cases of seven murdered Americans: the four churchwomen; journalist John Sullivan, who "disappeared" on December 28, 1980; and two land reform advisors, Michael Hammer and Mark Pearlman, shot in the coffee shop of the San Salvador Sheraton Hotel on January 3, 1980. Following congressional passage of that legislation, the Salvadoran National Guard undertook a limited investigation of the murders of Dorothy, Ita, Maura, and Jean.

Notwithstanding four U.S. presidential certifications over two years, little progress was made toward a trial in El Salvador until November 1983, when Congress passed a law withholding 30 percent of authorized military aid until there was a verdict in the case of the churchwomen. Preparations for a trial then progressed rapidly. In May 1984, the five National Guardsmen who apprehended the women on the night of December 2, 1980, were convicted of murder. This case marks the first time that members of the regular Salvadoran Security forces were convicted of a politically motivated murder, despite the fact that their victims number some 40,000 civilians since October 1979.

In the four years since the death of the missionaries, Church leaders in the United States have supported the families and religious communities in their pursuit of justice for the women and for the 40,000 other victims.

Since President Duarte assumed office in June 1984, he has established a commission to investigate five prominent cases: the murders of Archbishop Oscar Romero, John Sullivan, Michael Hammer, and Mark Pearlman, and the massacres in two villages in western El Salvador. The families and religious communities of Maura, Ita, Dorothy, and Jean intend to urge President Duarte to include a sixth case: that of the cover-up of the murder of the four women. A full investigation of the cover-up and the question of the involvement of higher officers in the crime has never been conducted. Attempts by the Clarke, Donovan, Ford, and Kazel families to gain access to FBI and State Department documents pertinent to the case under the Freedom of Information Act have not been successful. The agencies have vigorously resisted the families' attempts to obtain information. The few documents released by the FBI have been almost entirely excised (blacked out), thus making them useless as sources of information. Litigation continues, and the families and religious communities of Maura, Jean, Ita, and Dorothy pledge to pursue the investigation until the system of violence that has claimed more than 40,000 lives is finally exposed, and the killings brought to an end.

Afterword

MARGARET SWEDISH
Religious Task Force on Central America

1980 was a bloody year in El Salvador. Thousands of people were murdered by the military and the death squads—catechists, trade unionists, students, members of peasant organizations—as the country fell headlong into civil war.

The church was not spared. On March 24, Archbishop Oscar Arnulfo Romero was assassinated while celebrating Mass. He joined a growing list of church leaders and pastoral workers who had taken up the cause of the poor and suffered persecution and martyrdom because of it.

Despite his public defense of human rights as a hallmark of foreign policy, United States President Jimmy Carter gave way to his greater fear of a "leftist" insurrection threatening the Salvadoran government and, despite the urgent pleas of Monseñor Romero, increased military and security assistance to the military dictatorship that ruled at that time.

Ronald Reagan was elected president the following November. It was no secret anywhere in Latin America that the new administration would be much friendlier to the region's militaries. The message to El Salvador was clear—human rights would no longer be an impediment, rhetorical or otherwise, to the United States' full support for the military government.

It was in this period—the weeks of the Carter lame duck government, as power was shifted to the Salvadoran army's stauncher allies on the U.S. right—that the killing in El Salvador reached new bounds of outrage. Taking full advantage of this political "window of opportunity," the Salvadoran armed forces and their allied death squads committed a series of atrocities that clearly announced the new era.

On November 27, leaders of the Democratic Revolutionary Front (FDR), the most important group of opposition political leaders and perhaps El Salvador's last best hope of a political solution short of all-out war, were abducted from a Jesuit high school in which they were meeting and brutally assassinated.

As Salvadorans were burying their leaders on December 2, word came of the disappearance of four U.S. churchwomen, Maryknoll Sisters Maura Clark and Ita Ford, Cleveland Ursuline Sister Dorothy Kazel, and lay missioner Jean Donovan. Their bodies were found on December 4, buried in a shallow grave along an isolated road.

Later that month, U.S. journalist John Sullivan was assassinated. On January 3, so were Michael Hammer and Mark Pearlman, two U.S. advisors sent by the American Institute for Free Labor Development (AIFLD), the international arm of the AFL-CIO, to work on a government land reform program. Murdered with them was the director of the program, Rodolfo Viera.

In January guerrilla leaders of the Farabundo Martí National Liberation Front (FMLN), an alliance of five political-military factions, declared the beginning of a "final offensive." The Salvadoran army and security forces responded with a brutal counter-insurgency program, certain of the unqualified backing of their main sponsors in the United States. The FMLN was only one of the targets. Any opposition to the regime, no matter how legitimate or nonviolent, was put down with incredible brutality. Among the tens of thousands of Salvadorans who were slaughtered in the ensuing years were some of El Salvador's most gifted political, religious, and social leaders.

The civil war raged on for twelve years. In the end, most human rights organizations agree, about 75,000 Salvadorans were killed in the violence. The overwhelming majority of these deaths were attributed to the Salvadoran army. El Salvador's notorious death squads, linked institutionally and politically to the armed forces and certain leaders among the wealthy elite, placed an ignominious second among groups responsible for rights violations.

Besides the 75,000 dead, approximately 1 million Salvadorans ended up as refugees or displaced within their country. One-fifth of the population was forced to flee the terror in order to survive.

The United States sent over $6 billion in military and security aid during those years, and scores of military advisors who helped plan and direct the counterinsurgency strategy.

Part of the plan was to install a civilian-led government that would eventually hold elections and establish a civilian-based "democracy." It took several years before the U.S. government could convince the Salvadoran military leaders of the wisdom of this strategy. Presidential elections were held in 1984, and the winner was Christian Democrat José Napoleon Duarte, the choice of the U.S. government, which backed his candidacy politically and financially. The electoral exercise was severely criticized because of this intervention from outside and the conditions under which the elections were held—in the midst of war, boycotted by the left, and in a climate of severe repression. Duarte tried to implement a land reform program and pledged political reforms. He also held the very first peace talks with leaders of the FMLN and other opposition leaders. But the army was not yet interested in peace, and Duarte had only as much power as the military allowed him. There were few incentives for the army while military aid flowed from the United States. The war and repression raged on.

Presidential elections were held again in 1989. Alfredo Cristiani, candidate of the Nationalist Republican Alliance (ARENA), emerged triumphant as the Christian Democrat Party (PDC) fell into disrepute for its association with the counterinsurgency war and because of rampant corruption in the PDC government.

Cristiani's ARENA party was founded by cashiered Major Roberto D'Aubuisson, a reputed founder and organizer of the death squads. It was created to provide a political vehicle for the right, to gain international legitimacy through participation in the formal democratic process. For U.S. strategists, this was a key component of the campaign to defeat the FMLN politically as well as militarily, robbing the insurgents and their supporters of political credibility.

The climate for the 1989 elections was not vastly different from 1984. Human rights violations had decreased numerically, in part because the campaign of killing had been so effective. On the other hand, the army had been waging a fierce air war in the countryside, and hundreds of thousands of potential voters sympathetic to the left were outside the country as refugees or displaced within it, almost all of them without identity papers. The threat of repression was as real as ever—impunity for rights violators remained nearly total.

But ARENA was not a monolithic organization. It suffered internal strains between those loyal to the D'Aubuisson legacy, who believed the only way to deal with the insurgency and the threat of "communism" once and for all was to destroy the FMLN and its supporters, and a more "pragmatic" sector led by Cristiani, who believed the battle was also political and social—not just a military battle for total annihilation of "the enemy," but a war for "the hearts and minds" of the population and the international community.

The Cristiani presidency represented the dominance of this sector within ARENA and the strategy of the U.S. government.

While divided over the means, ARENA was still united in its determination to defeat the FMLN. During the late 1980s, the guerrillas had slowly rebuilt their ranks and capacity after the decimation suffered during the army's rampage of the early part of the decade. Faced with an ARENA government supported unquestioningly by the United States, FMLN strategists believed it was time to show their renewed strength. On November 11, 1989, they launched a massive offensive in several parts of the country, most notably in the capital city of San Salvador, which had seen little of the civil war's military battles. They quickly took over several neighborhoods in which they had been quietly organizing for years.

The army responded with bombing and strafing that killed hundreds of civilians and terrified the population. The FMLN was eventually forced to retreat from the capital, in part because of the cost being borne by the civilian population, but it was clear that the FMLN could continue the war indefinitely.

This was one factor that finally led to the negotiating table. It was clear that the U.S. was growing tired of the war, especially the U.S. Congress, which held the purse strings and was worn down by the endless battles over military aid. With the Cold War no longer a major factor in U.S. foreign policy, there was no ideological justification for aiding El Salvador's military.

But another, far more powerful impetus brought the Salvadoran government to the table and caused the administration of George Bush, Reagan's successor, to finally put the weight of the U.S. government behind the talks. Just five days into the FMLN's offensive, on November 16, 1989, members of the elite U.S.-trained Atlacatl Battalion entered the campus of the Jesuit Central

America University and assassinated six Jesuits, their housekeeper, and her daughter.

The decision to carry out the assassinations had been made the previous evening during a meeting of the Armed Forces High Command. Among those who gave the orders was General René Emilio Ponce, Minister of Defense and close ally of the U.S. government. In fact, the Bush administration saw him as key to the image of reform and "modernization" of the military that was the focus of its campaign to sell its policy in El Salvador.

The ruthlessness of these assassinations and the subsequent cover-up in which the United States participated revealed in stark terms a fundamental fact about El Salvador: the structures of institutionalized repression and the impunity that protected it were still intact, despite elections that had brought two successive civilian governments to the presidency and ended the formal mechanisms of military dictatorship.

In January 1992, at Chapultepec, Mexico, the Salvadoran government and the FMLN signed peace accords that formally ended the war. The accords focused on political and military reforms that were intended to open political space for the FMLN and its combatants to lay down their arms, form a political party, and reintegrate into Salvadoran society. They established mechanisms to guarantee their security and provide at least minimal resources for former combatants on both sides—and the FMLN's social base, populations displaced during the war—to be able to survive. These resources included land, technical training, and production credits.

The military's various security forces—the National Guard, Treasury Police, National Police—and several elite army battalions known for their record of rights abuses were to be dissolved. The army was to be purged of rights violators. A United Nations Truth Commission was established, charged with looking into the country's most egregious rights abuses, such as the assassinations of Romero, the four U.S. churchwomen, and the UCA massacre, and establishing responsibility for those acts.

The accords called for a complete overhaul of the judicial system as a key component to ending impunity. It also created a new National Civilian Police (PNC) that was to be under civilian authority and protected from becoming a new instrument of repression. Recruits would be made up in the following proportions: no more than 20 percent from former FMLN ranks, no more than 20 percent from former military ranks, and the other 60 percent from those not associated with either side in the war. There would be special training in respect for human rights and the treatment of citizens. As the PNC was trained and deployed, the old militarized National Police would be dissolved.

The process of monitoring and verifying compliance with the accords was put in the hands of the United Nations.

While these reforms still did not get at the roots of El Salvador's civil war—its deeply entrenched structures of economic injustice expressed in profoundly concentrated wealth among a small elite—they provided the means for the struggle for justice to move from war to the political arena in an atmosphere free of repression, where basic political rights such as free speech and association would be respected.

Three years after the signing of these accords, El Salvador remained a deeply wounded, traumatized country. The consequences of such brutal warfare have been profound: damage to the psyches and spirits of the people; devastation of the country's environment and economy, which will plague its efforts at reconstruction and development for years to come; tensions and divisions within its main political players such as the Christian Democrats, ARENA, and the FMLN as political leaders vie for power and position within the new political context; resistance of the elites and the military to reforms that would seriously undermine their economic and political power.

And what was won at the peace table has not necessarily been consolidated in the "new" El Salvador. Several FMLN leaders were assassinated in the three years following the signing of the accords. In most cases, the government claimed it was common crime. As of this writing, no one has been prosecuted or convicted in these cases.

In 1994 the National Civilian Police, a key pillar in the process of ending structural violence, received the dubious honor of becoming the main target of human rights complaints, according to the Human Rights Division of the UN's monitoring mission.

The land transfer program and programs for the reintegration of former combatants remained far behind schedule by late 1994. Growing frustrations fueled increasingly militant and violent protests from former combatants, especially army soldiers and members of the dissolved security forces.

In the countryside where communities were to receive the benefits of the land transfer program, the government's failure to comply with its commitments is drawing concern over the potential for future "social explosions." This is especially true in those areas formerly controlled by the FMLN where populations are highly *conscientized*, have great organizing capacity, and are increasingly disillusioned at the outcome of the war—and the peace.

Judicial reform, another key component in the struggle to end impunity, also remains far from the goals set by the UN. Rights violators continue to act with impunity, protected by a judicial system fraught with corruption, indifference to human rights, or complicity with rights violators.

The structure of the death squads also remains intact. The UN considers these structures responsible for much of the rapidly rising organized crime activity, while saying they are still available to commit acts of political violence when called upon to do so. In October 1994, UN Secretary General Boutros Boutros-Ghali called on the government to dismantle the death squads. But El Salvador's newly elected ARENA president, Armando Calderon Sol, installed in June 1994, has shown little commitment to do so, and in fact was implicated in death squad activity in the early 1980s.

While this picture appears grim, there is something else that is true about El Salvador. The civil war came about because the popular expression of the people who had been organizing throughout the 1960s and 1970s had been frustrated and fiercely repressed. Civil war did not bring about, and probably in the end never could have brought about, the fulfillment of all their hopes.

But what so many people did learn was a new sense of their own dignity and worth—a revolutionary change in consciousness for a region in which the poor had long been told to merely accept their lot and await their reward in heaven. They learned to believe in themselves, to be able to look at their world and evaluate it critically, to understand the causes and roots of their suffering.

They learned organizing skills, developed a capacity for popular education, alternative forms of health promotion, how to work together in communities, how to share and sacrifice in order to move forward in the long process of liberation.

They had with them during those decades of organizing and *conscientización* (the process of developing critical consciousness) a Church that had decided to immerse itself in their world and be on their side in the search for justice. Monseñor Romero, the four U.S. churchwomen, and the UCA Jesuit martyrs were among those who incarnated that mission of accompaniment of a people in search of their own liberation from oppression and poverty.

But the fruits of those years of struggle were not born in El Salvador alone. The sacrifice of the martyrs of El Salvador, the witness of their lives and deaths, gave birth to a solidarity in the United States and other parts of the world that continues to animate the thirst for justice in literally thousands of communities of faith. The experience of many U.S. citizens in encountering the martyred nation of El Salvador has been described over and over again as conversion, as if seeing and living the gospel of Jesus Christ for the first time.

The story of what leads people to give their lives for others is the essence of the Gospel story. In that sense, the stories told in this volume of Maryknoll Sisters Maura Clark, Ita Ford, and Carla Piette are a profound expression of that gospel for our time. Their witness, and that of Dorothy Kazel and Jean Donovan, these wonderful women who came from us and in martyrdom are given back to us, are repositories of hope, a fierce and active hope pointing the way to how this world, this suffering, this martyrdom in El Salvador will be transformed into redemption for our world. They show us the meaning of incarnation by having incarnated their faith, their hope, in that moment, that reality, in El Salvador. By doing so, they also show us what it means to incarnate *our* faith and hope at this time in our world. They join us together in the long struggle for liberation with the people of El Salvador, Nicaragua, Chile, and all the poor of our world.

Appendix 1

From Madness to Hope

The 12-year war in El Salvador

Excerpt from the Report of the Commission on the Truth for El Salvador
March 1993

(c) THE AMERICAN CHURCHWOMEN

SUMMARY OF THE CASE

On 2 December 1980, members of the National Guard of El Salvador arrested four church women after they left the international airport. Churchwomen Ita Ford, Maura Clarke, Dorothy Kazel and Jean Donovan were taken to an isolated spot and subsequently executed by being shot at close range.

In 1984, Deputy Sergeant Luis Antonio Colindres Alemán and National Guard members Daniel Canales Ramírez, Carlos Joaquín Conteras Palacios, Francisco Orlando Conteras Recinos and José Roberto Moreno Canjura were sentenced to 30 years in prison for murder.

The Commission on the Truth finds that:

1. The arrest and execution of the churchwomen was planned prior to their arrival at the airport. Deputy Sergeant Luis Antonio Colindres Alemán carried out the orders of a superior to execute them.

2. Then Colonel Carlos Eugenio Vides Casanova, Director-General of the National Guard, Lieutenant Colonel Oscar Edgardo Casanova Vejar, Commander of the Zacatecoluca military detach-

ment, Colonel Roberto Monterrosa, Major Lizandro Zepeda Velasco and Sergeant Dagoberto Martínez, among other military personnel, knew that members of the National Guard had committed the murders pursuant to orders of a superior. The subsequent cover-up of the facts adversely affected the judicial investigation process.

3. The Minister of Defense at the time, General José Guillermo García, made no serious attempt to conduct a thorough investigation of responsibility for the murders.

4. Local Commissioner José Dolores Meléndez also knew of the executions carried out by members of the security forces and covered them up.

5. The State of El Salvador failed in its responsibility to investigate the facts thoroughly, to find the culprits and to punish them in accordance with the law and the requirements of international human rights law.

DESCRIPTION OF THE FACTS[1]

THE MURDERS

Shortly after 7 P.M. on 2 December 1980, members of the National Guard of El Salvador arrested four churchwomen as they were leaving Comalapa International Airport. Churchwomen Ita Ford, Maura Clarke, Dorothy Kazel and Jean Donovan were taken to an isolated spot where they were shot dead at close range.

Two of the four murdered churchwomen, Ita Ford and Maura Clarke, worked in Chalatenango and were returning from Nicaragua. The other two had come from La Libertad to pick them up at the airport.

The arrests were planned in advance. Approximately two hours before the churchwomen's arrival, National Guard Deputy Sergeant Luis Antonio Colindres Alemán informed five of his subordinates that they were to arrest some people who were coming from Nicaragua.

Colindres then went to San Luis Talpa command post to warn the commander that, if he heard some disturbing noises, he should ignore them, because they would be the result of an action which Colindres and his men would be carrying out.

Once the members of the security force had brought the churchwomen to an isolated place, Colindres returned to his post

near the airport. On returning to the place where they had taken
the churchwomen he told his men that he had been given orders
to kill the churchwomen.

THE INVESTIGATION

1. *The Burial*

The next morning, 3 December, the bodies were found on the
road. When the justice of the peace arrived, he immediately agreed
that they should be buried, as local commissioner José Dolores
Meléndez had indicated. Accordingly, local residents buried the
churchwomen's bodies in the vicinity.

The United States Ambassador, Robert White, found out on 4
December where the churchwomen's bodies were. As a result of
his intervention and once authorization had been obtained from the
justice of the peace, the corpses were exhumed and taken to San
Salvador. There a group of forensic doctors refused to perform
autopsies on the grounds that they had no surgical masks.

2. *The Rogers-Bowdler mission*

Between 6 and 9 December 1980, a special mission arrived in
San Salvador, headed by Mr. William D. Rogers, a former official
in the Administration of President Gerald Ford, and Mr. William
G. Bowdler, a state department official.

They found no direct evidence of the crime, nor any evidence
implicating the Salvadorian authorities. They concluded that the
operation had involved a cover-up of the murders.[2]

They also urged the Federal Bureau of investigation (FBI) to
play an active role in the investigation.[3]

3. *The Monterrosa commission and the Zepeda investigation*

The Government Junta put Colonel Roberto Monterrosa in
charge of an official commission of investigation. Colonel Carlos
Eugenio Vides Casanova, Director-General of the National Guard,
put Major Lizandro Zepeda[4] in charge of another investigation.
Neither official took the case seriously or sought to resolve it.
Subsequently, Judge Harold R. Tyler, Jr., appointed by the United
States Secretary of State, carried out a third investigation. It found

that the purpose of the two previous investigations had been to establish a written precedent clearing the Salvadorian security forces of blame for the killings.[5]

(a) *The Monterrosa commission*

Colonel Monterrosa admitted that his commission had ruled out the possibility that security forces had been involved in the crime; to have acknowledged it would have created serious difficulties for the armed forces.

In fact, Monterrosa kept back the evidence implicating Colindres. In February 1981, he sent the United States Embassy the fingerprints of three out of four National Guard members from whom the commission had taken statements. However, none of them appeared to have been involved in the murders. Colonel Monterrosa failed to provide the fingerprints of the fourth man, Colindres, from whom testimony had also apparently been taken. Judge Tyler therefore concluded that Colonel Monterrosa had not forwarded Colindres' fingerprints because he knew from Major Zepeda that Colindres was responsible for the executions.[6]

(b) *The Zepeda investigation*

Major Zepeda reported that there was no evidence that members of the National Guard had executed the churchwomen.[7]

According to testimony Major Zepeda personally took charge of covering up for the murderers by ordering them to replace their rifles so as not to be detected, and to remain loyal to the National Guard by suppressing the facts.

There is also sufficient evidence that Major Zepeda informed his superior, Vides Casanova, of his activities.[8]

4. *Resolution of the Case*

In April 1981,[9] the United States Embassy provided the Salvadorian authorities with evidence incriminating Colindres and his men. Despite the existence of evidence against Colindres, such as the presence of his fingerprints on the churchwomen's minibus, neither he nor his subordinates were charged with any crime.[10]

In December 1981, Colonel Vides Casanova appointed Major José Adolfo Medrano to carry out a new investigation. In February 1982, one of the persons involved confessed his guilt and implicated the others, including Colindres. All of them were charged with the deaths of the churchwomen.

On 10 February, President Duarte in a televised message reported that the case had been resolved. He also gave to understand that Colindres and his men had acted independently and not on orders of a superior. In conclusion he said that the Government was convinced that the accused were guilty.[11]

THE JUDICIAL PROCESS

1. The judicial investigation

The judicial investigation did not represent any substantial progress over what the Medrano working group had done. Nevertheless, under questioning by the FBI, Sergeant Dagoberto Martínez, then Colindres' immediate superior, admitted to having been told by Colindres himself about the churchwomen's murders and about his direct role in them. On that occasion, Martínez had warned Colindres not to say anything unless his superiors asked him about it. Martínez also said that he had not been aware that orders had been given by a superior.[12]

2. The trial

On 23 and 24 May 1984, members of the National Guard were found guilty of the executions of the churchwomen and were sentenced to 30 years in prison.[13]

It was the first time in Salvadorian history that a member of the armed forces had been convicted of murder by a judge.[14]

Despite ambiguous statements by some of its official representatives,[15] the United States Government had made its economic and military aid contingent on a resolution of the case.[16]

The involvement of senior officers

Although the Tyler report concluded in 1983, ". . . based on existing evidence,"[17] that senior officers had not been involved, the commission believes that there is sufficient evidence to show that Colindres acted on orders of a superior.

There is also substantial evidence that Lieutenant Colonel

Oscar Edgardo Casanova Vejar, Commander of the Zacatecoluca detachment, was in charge of the National Guard at the national airport at the time when the murders of the churchwomen occurred.

General Vides Casanova and Colonel Casanova Vejar have denied any personal involvement in the arrest and execution or in the subsequent cover-up of the crime. Nevertheless, there is sufficient evidence to show that both General Vides Casanova and Colonel Casanova Vejar knew that members of the National Guard had murdered the churchwomen, and that their efforts to impede the gathering of evidence adversely affected the judicial investigation.

Cooperation with the Commission on the Truth

On several occasions from October 1992 onwards, the judge of the First Criminal Court of Zacatecoluca, Mr. Pleitus Lemus, refused to cooperate with the Commission on the Truth and to provide the evidence and the full court dossiers of the case. He transmitted only a condensed version which does not include testimony and other critical evidence on the possible involvement of senior officers in the case.

It was only after much insisting that, in January 1993, the commission finally obtained all the dossiers of the case from the Supreme Court, barely a week before its mandate expired.

FINDINGS

The Commission on the Truth finds that:

1. There is sufficient evidence that:

(a) The arrest of the churchwomen at the airport was planned prior to their arrival.

(b) In arresting and executing the four churchwomen, Deputy Sergeant Luis Antonio Colindres Alemán was acting on orders of a superior.

2. There is substantial evidence that:

(a) Then Colonel Carlos Eugenio Vides Casanova, Director-General of the National Guard, Lieutenant Colonel Oscar Edgardo Casanova Vejar, Commander of the Zacatecoluca military detachment, Colonel Roberto Monterrosa, Major Lizandro Zapeda Velasco and Sergeant Dagoberto Martínez, among other officers, knew that members of the National Guard had committed the murders and, through their actions, facilitated the cover-up of the facts which obstructed the corresponding judicial investigation.

(b) The Minister of Defense at the time, General José Guillermo García made no serious effort to conduct a thorough investigation of responsibility for the murders of the churchwomen.

(c) Local Commissioner José Dolores Meléndez also knew of the murders and covered up for the members of the security forces who committed them.

3. The State of El Salvador failed in its obligation under international rights law to investigate the case, to bring to trial those responsible for ordering and carrying out the executions and, lastly, to compensate the victims' relatives.

Appendix 2

Excerpt from the Report of the Secretary of State's Panel on El Salvador

July 1993

George S. Vest, Member, Career Ambassador, Ret.
Richard W. Murphy, Member, Career Ambassador, Ret.
I.M. Destler, Academic Advisor, Professor, University of
Maryland

[. . .]

4. MURDER OF FOUR AMERICAN CHURCHWOMEN

On December 2, 1980, members of the Salvadoran National Guard arrested four American churchwomen (nuns Ita Ford, Maura Clarke and Dorothy Kazel, and laywoman Jean Donovan) on a road from the international airport. They were taken to an isolated spot, raped and killed. In 1984, Sergeant Luis Antonio Colindres Aleman and four other members of the National Guard were sentenced to thirty years for the crime. The *Truth Commission* concluded the abductions were planned in advance and the men had carried out the murders on orders from above. It further stated that the head of the National Guard and two officers assigned to investigate the case had concealed the facts to harm the judicial process.

This particular act of barbarism and attempts by the Salvadoran

military to cover it up did more to inflame the debate over El
Salvador in the United States than any other single incident. It
produced a grass-roots opposition to the incoming Administration's
El Salvador policy. The comments by UN Ambassador-designate
Jeanne Kirkpatrick in December and Secretary of State Haig in
March on the churchwomen's motives and the event itself were
taken as "emblematic" of the Reagan Administration's approach
on human rights in El Salvador.* Congressional interest was intense and books and a television documentary added to the public
controversy on the issue.

Embassy involvement in the case was strong from the beginning. The Ambassador went immediately to the temporary burial
site of the women, the Embassy human rights officer broke the
case, and the perpetrators were brought to justice only after intense
pressures from both the Executive branch and Congress. In the
midst of continuing public debate, Secretary Schultz asked Judge
Harold R. Tyler, Jr. to make an independent investigation in 1983.
His highly detailed study concluded that the National Guardsmen
were indeed guilty, that an extensive cover-up had occurred, and
that "the killers would never have been identified and the evidence
of their guilt never properly assembled had it not been for the
efforts, often courageous, of the United States (State Department

---

*. . . Professor [Jeanne] Kirkpatrick, who became the Reagan Administration's
Ambassador to the United Nations and an important player on Central American
issues, was quoted in the *Tampa Tribune* of December 25, 1980, as having said on
December 16: "I don't think that the government was responsible. The nuns were
not just nuns; the nuns were political activists. We ought to be a little more clear-cut
about this than we usually are. They were political activists on behalf of the Front,
and somebody who is using violence to oppose the Front killed them." She later
said this was a misquote, that she had said the nuns "were perceived by people in
El Salvador as political activists." Secretary of State Haig told the House Foreign
Affairs Committee in March 1981: "I would like to suggest to you that some of the
investigations would lead one to believe that perhaps the vehicle that the nuns were
riding in may have tried to run a roadblock or may have accidentally been perceived
to have been doing so, and there may have been an exchange of fire." The
assumption of several of the people interviewed was that the Secretary must have
seen some speculation in raw intelligence data or a cover story by some in the
Salvadoran military. They had not seen the reference themselves. The statement
was a clear mistake which should have been labeled as such immediately.

and FBI) personnel." Unlike the Truth Commission, Judge Tyler concluded that Colindres Aleman probably acted on his own initiative.

Embassy reporting and the files of this key case are extensive. After the first visit to the exhumation site and discussions with local officials, the Embassy reported that the implication that the churchwomen were murdered by Salvadoran security officials was "absolutely clear." The U.S. sent William D. Rogers and assistant secretary Bowdler to El Salvador to make an immediate appraisal and underline the importance the U.S. attached to a prompt and thorough investigation. They found no direct evidence implicating Salvadoran authorities and urged that the FBI play a role in the investigation. The junto announced that Colonel Roberto Monterrosa would conduct an investigation into the crime and the National Police initiated a separate effort led by Major Lizandro Zepeda.

The Monterrosa Commission originally appeared to the Embassy to be sincere and "pursuing every avenue to bring this matter to a logical conclusion." After it took a long Christmas break and then proceeded at a much slower pace in January, however, the Embassy was much less confident about prospects for progress. On January 19th Ambassador White took issue with statements from Washington that the investigation was proceeding satisfactorily, saying that there was "no sign of any sincere attempt to locate and punish those responsible for this atrocity." In fact, as Judge Tyler stated, "Colonel Monterrosa did as little as possible throughout the early spring of 1981," despite instructions to the contrary from President Duarte. Monterrosa clearly knew what he was doing.

When, after much prodding, he provided fingerprints to the U.S. in February of three of the four people from whom his Commission had taken statements, he specifically omitted prints from the person responsible.

Meanwhile, the U.S. Embassy was pressing its own effort. A contact of the human rights officer told him in April that Subsergeant Colindres Aleman had ordered the murders. Chargé Chapin met separately with President Duarte and Minister of Defense Garcia to tell them of this information, noting specifically that Colindres' fingerprints had not been passed to the Embassy by Monterrosa. Garcia promised the guilty would be punished. In discussions over the next few days, the source provided the names of all those involved and these too were formally handed over to the minister for action. The people on the Embassy's list were arrested the next day, their fingerprints taken, and guns sent to the U.S. for analysis. The FBI soon identified Colindres' print as matching one on the churchwomen's van and one of the confiscated rifles as having fired a shell discovered at the scene of the crime.

As the issue languished through the Fall, the Embassy pressed hard for a serious follow-up investigation. Then in December the National Guard established a new working group headed by Major Jose Adolfo Medrano to carry out an investigation. Medrano's group carried out a much more serious effort with direct Embassy involvement and technical assistance from the FBI. The Embassy reported the developments in the case in considerable detail. The Medrano investigation was completed on February 9, 1982. President Duarte announced the resolution of the case the next day, and the six men were discharged from the National Guard and turned over to civilian authorities for trial.

The process again slowed as the civilian authorities tarried in carrying out their investigation. Tensions over the case in the United States grew as predicted trial dates were not met. The frustrations of the families and their supporters grew apace. Some charged that: a) progress was not being made as required by the certification legislation, b) the U.S. was assisting the delay ("there is mounting evidence that both responsible officials of El Salvador and what is more appalling, officials of the murdered women's own government, are studiously avoiding the measures that might expose the truth," said one critical report), c) the Administration was ignoring "evidence indicating that higher military officials participated in ordering the crime and covering it up,"and d) the U.S. Government refused to declassify all information it had for the families and their supporters to use.

Questions were raised about leads not followed or facts ignored that suggested a conspiracy. The investigation by Judge Tyler was designed to spur on the Salvadoran justice system and to review the merit of the many accusations and theories being advanced by the critics. His study, completed on December 2, 1983, and declassified following the verdict in the trial, took strong exception to criticism of the Department's role, noting its and the FBI representatives had been "vigorous and effective" in pressing the Salvadorans to investigate and prosecute the crime.

With the U.S. pressure intense, the Salvadorans moved the case to the trial stage in October. Finally, on May 26, 1984, the defendants were found guilty and sentenced to 30 years in prison. The Truth Commission noted that this was the first time in Salvadoran history that a judge had found a member of the military guilty of assassination. Those convicted filed a petition for release under the November 5, 1988, amnesty. This was denied after the judge ruled that the killings were not a political crime, therefore not covered by the amnesty.

Notes

1. A Common Grave

1. Teresa Alexander MM, and Madeline Dorsey MM, tape to Maryknoll Sisters Community, 6 December 1980, Maryknoll Sisters' Archives MSA: I C; and tape to Ford family, 6 December 1980, MSA: I E.

2. Chile

1. Jackie Hansen Maggiore, letter to Judith M. Noone MM (JMN), 18 August 1982, MSA: 2 A.

2. "Pre-Profession Opinion," Confidential File, MSA: 3 A.

3. Mary Ellen Manz MM, interview with JMN. 6 May 1982, MSA: 4 D.

4. Ibid.

5. Carla Piette MM, letter to Mrs. Jack Frazier, 7 October 1967, MSA: C 13.

6. "The Chilean Experiment," 1969, MSA: C c.

7. Manz, MSA: 4 D.

8. 2 October 1966, MSA: C 7.

9. 2 September 1967, MSA: C 11.

10. 11 August 1971, MSA: C 16.

11. Letter to Barbara Hendricks MM, 21 May 1972, MSA: C 20.

12. 3 August 1974, MSA: C 25.

3. Searching

1. Mrs. Mildred Ford, letter to JMN, Summer 1981, MSA: 11 D.

2. Ita Ford MM, letter to Jean Rearden, 17 March 1961, MSA: 18. (Unless otherwise designated, all letters from Ita in this chapter are to Jean Rearden.)

3. 19 April 1961, MSA: I 11.

4. 8 November 1961, MSA: I 15.

5. Ibid.

6. Ibid.

7. Ibid.

8. 7 January 1962, MSA: I 18.

9. 28 February 1962, MSA: I 20.

10. 30 December 1962, MSA: I 27; and 18 August 1963, MSA: I 31.

11. 26 January 1964, MSA: I 35.

12. 12 April 1964, MSA: I 36.

13. 12 June 1964, MSA: I 37.

14. MSA: I 38.

15. Mrs. Mildred Ford, letter to JMN, 28 January 1982, MSA: 11 A.

16. Letter to Mary Galligan MM, 10 September 1964, MSA: I 39.

17. Kathleen Monahan Gregg and Ana May, interview with JMN, 24 April 1981, MSA: 11 C.

18. Julie Miller MM, letter to JMN, 14 February 1982, MSA: 13 A.

4. State of Siege

1. Ita Ford MM, letter to Jean Rearden, 6 October 1971, MSA: I 44. (Unless otherwise designated, letters from Ita in this chapter are to Jean Rearden.)

2. Ibid.

3. Easter Week 1972, MSA: I 46.

4. Ibid.

5. 24 September 1972, MSA: I 48.

6. Ibid.

7. 28 November 1972, MSA: I 50.

8. 10 March 1973, MSA: I 54.

9. 23 May 1973, MSA: I 57.

10. Ibid.

11. Letter to Kathleen Monahan Gregg and her husband, Michael, 9 June 1973, MSA: I 58.

12. 12 August 1973, MSA: I 60.

13. Constance Pospisil MM, interview with JMN, 22 April 1982, MSA: 4 E.

14. Ibid.

5. Carla and Ita

1. Carla Piette MM, "*Poblacion La Bandera*," 1974, MSA: C a.

2. Ita Ford MM, interview with Maureen Flanagan, Maryknoll Sisters' Communications Office, 1978, MSA: I c.

3. Carla Piette MM, letter to Mr. and Mrs. Jack Frazier, 3 August 1974, MSA: C 25.

4. Carla Piette MM, "What Have I Learned?", 1974, MSA: C b.

5. Flanagan interview, MSA: I c.

6. *Medellín Conclusiones* (Bogota: Secretariado General del CELAM, 1976); English translation published by the U.S. Catholic Conference.

7. Ibid.

8. Letter to Jean Rearden Baumann and her husband, John, MSA: I 67.

9. Constance Pospisil MM, interview with JMN, 22 April 1982, MSA: 4 E. (Until the next footnote, all quotes are from this interview.)

10. Ita Ford MM (and Carla Piette?), "Try to imagine . . ." 1975?, MSA: 4 H.

11. Episcopado Chileno, Comite Permanente, "Evangelio y Paz," (September 1975), *Mensaje* 24 (October 1975).

12. Sheila Cassidy, tape to Mrs. Mildred Ford, May 1981, MSA: 4 B.

13. 20 September 1976, MSA: C 30.

14. Letter to Jean Rearden Baumann, 28 November 1977, MSA: I 75.

15. Pospisil, MSA: 4 E.

16. Letter to Jean Baumann, 28 November 1977, MSA: I 75.

17. "Bolivian Government Plan Against The Church," *Latin America Documentation* (Washington, D.C: U.S. Catholic Conference, June 1975), pp. 1-4.

18. Rachel Lauze MM, letter to JMN, 21 January 1982, MSA: 10 A.

19. Mrs. Mildred Ford, letter to JMN, 28 January 1982, MSA: 11 A.

20. John Patrick Meehan MM, letter to JMN, 1 May 1981, MSA: 10 B.

21. Letter to Constance Pospisil MM, 21 June 1978, MSA: I 77.

22. Patricia Haggerty MM, interview with JMN, 17 June 1981, MSA: 16 C.

6. Maura

1. A two-page autobiography written in Spanish, probably in Nicaragua before December 1972, MSA: 6 D.

2. John and Mary Clarke, interview with Margaret Dillon MM, 28 September 1982, MSA: 20 A.

3. Mary Clarke, interview with JMN, 30 September 1982, MSA: 20 B.

4. Maura Clarke, her application to join the Maryknoll Sisters, 1949, MSA: 20 C.

5. Ibid.

6. Ibid.

7. Jimmy Breslin, "Maura's Dead and It's a Crime," *Daily News*, 7 December 1980, MSA: 20 D.

8. Autobiography, MSA: 6 D.

9. Richard Marie McKinney MM, interview with JMN, 2 August 1982, MSA: 21 A.

10. Ibid.

11. Marie Rosso MM, interview with JMN, August 1982, MSA: 21 B.

12. "Final Profession Opinion," Confidential File, MSA: 3 B.

13. Robert Armbruster, "Sisters To The World," *Sign* (July/August 1980), pp. 24-25.

7. Siuna

1. Siuna Diary, 1944, MSA: 5 A. (Until the next footnote, quotes are from this source.)

2. "Maryknoll Sisters' Efforts to Combat Hunger," Supplementary Report to the Mission Secretariate, Washington, D.C., March 1966, MSA: 5 B.

3. Christmas 1963, MSA: M 9.

4. Mary Clarke, interview with JMN, MSA: 20 B.

5. Laura Glynn MM, letter to JMN, 30 September 1982, MSA: 6 E.

6. Ibid.

7. 6 August 1967, MSA: M 17.

8. MSA: M 21.

9. MSA: M 19.

10. 9 September 1968, MSA: M 22.

11. "Report on Siuna (Nicaragua) Dam Break." Mission News Service, Maryknoll, N.Y., MSA: 5 C.

12. Ibid.

13. "Conclusions of House Records of the Siuna Mission," 16 December 1968, MSA: 5 D.

14. Beatrice Zaragoza MM, tape to JMN, August 1982, MSA: 6 1.

8. Earthquake

1. Julia Clarke Keogh, interview with JMN, 26 July 1982, MSA: 20 E.

2. Palm Sunday 1970, MSA: M 32a.

3. 15 October 1970, MSA: M 44.

4. Letter to her parents, 12 October 1970, MSA: M 43.

5. Letter to "Family and Friends," Christmas 1971, MSA: M 64.

6. Letter to her family, 6 July 1973, MSA: M 88.

7. Letter to Julia Clarke Keogh, October (?) 1972, MSA: M 70.

8. Melba Bantay Gierlach, tape to JMN, July 1982, MSA: 8 B; and Maura Clarke MM, letter to her parents, 25 December 1972, MSA: M 75.

9. 25 December 1972, MSA: M 75.

10. Ibid.

11. 18 March 1973, MSA: M 80.

9. Signs of Struggle

1. Geraldine Brake MM, interview with JMN, 17 August 1982, MSA: 6 F.

2. Letter to "Family and Friends," Christmas 1974, MSA: M 124.

3. 9 June 1974, MSA: M 108.

4. Margaret Dillon MM, interview with JMN, 26 July 1982, MSA: 6 G.

5. 16 July 1976, MSA: M 157.

6. 29 April 1976, MSA: M 157; and 7 October 1976, MSA: M 160.

7. MSA: M b.

8. Maryknoll Sisters Maria Rieckelman, Melba Bantay, and Margarita Jamias, *Eulogy for Maura Clarke*, 12 December 1980, MSA: 8 A.

10. Solidarity

1. "Proceedings of the 11th General Assembly, Maryknoll Sisters, Maryknoll, New York, October 15-December 2, 1978," MSA: 9 A.

2. *Providence Visitor*, 30 November 1978.

3. Eucharista Coupe MM, interview with JMN, 15 March 1983, MSA: 7 D.

4. *Central Board Communique*, Maryknoll Sisters, March/April 1978, MSA: 7 D.

5. Constance Pospisil MM, letter to JMN, 31 May 1981. MSA: 4 F.

11. A Poor Old Beggar

1. Ita Ford MM, "Annual Evaluation, Reflection Year," May 1979, MSA: 10 D; and I 78.

2. John Patrick Meehan MM, letter to JMN, 1 May 1981. MSA: 10 B.

3. 17 July 1979, MSA: I 79.

4. "Maryknoll Sisters in Nicaragua, August 1979," MSA: 12 A.

5. Dan Driscoll MM, interview with JMN, February 1982, MSA: 8 C.

6. Pages from a notebook, "Trip to Ireland, 5 August 1979," MSA: M 174.

7. MSA: I 79.

8. MSA: 12 A.

9. 16 November 1979, MSA: C43 a.

10. "Reflections On The Mission Phase," May 1977, MSA: 171.

11. Julie Miller MM, letter to JMN, 14 February 1982, MSA: 13 A.

12. Ibid.

13. Rebecca Quinn MM, interview with JMN, 16 February 1983, MSA: 4 G.

14. 21 January 1980, MSA: C 50.

15. 10 February 1980, MSA: 183.

16. Letter to the Sisters in Chile, 1 February 1980, MSA: C 52.

17. Ibid.

12. A Shepherd's Sacrifice

1. Letter to the Sisters in Chile, 1 February 1980, MSA: C 52.

2. Letter to Cecelia Vandal MM, 14 May, 1980, MSA: C 73.

3. Letter to Betty and Jack Frazier, 27 March 1980, MSA: C 55.

4. Letter to the Sisters in Chile, 20 March 1980, MSA: C 53.

5. Vandal, MSA: C 73.

6. Letter to Mrs. Mildred Ford, 2 March 1980. MSA: I 87.

7. Letter to "Dear Family and Friends," Christmas 1979, MSA: M 177.

8. Letter to Jennie Burke MM. 15 January 1980, MSA: M 178.

9. Placido Erdozain, *Archbishop Romero, Martyr of Salvador* (Maryknoll, New York: Orbis Books, 1981), pp. 73-74.

10. Ibid, pp. 77-79.

11. Ibid.

12. Ibid, p. 75.

13. 28 March 1980, MSA: 15 C.

14. James R. Brockman, *The Word Remains: A Life of Oscar Romero* (Maryknoll, New York: Orbis Books, 1982), pp. 216-217.

15. Ibid.

16. Sisters of the PANISA Region, "Reflections on Recent Events," 14 April 1980, MSA: 15 E.

17. 26 March 1980, MSA: C 54.

18. Letter to Rebecca Quinn MM, 28 March 1980, MSA: C 56.

19. Ibid.

20. MSA: 15 E.

21. Ibid.

22. Ibid.

23. 2 April 1980, MSA: 188.

24. Madeline Dorsey MM, interview with JMN, 26 February 1983, MSA: 16 J.

25. 13 April 1980, MSA: I 89.

26. Julie Miller MM, letter to JMN, 14 February 1982, MSA: 13 A.

13. "Lord of the Impossible"

1. Carla Piette and Ita Ford MM, "Three Months' Experience In El Salvador," 20 July 1980, MSA: 17 C.

2. Ita Ford and Carla Piette MM, letter to Regina McEvoy MM, 3 May 1980, MSA: I 96.

3. Christine Rody VSC interview with Joan Petrik MM, summer 1981, MSA: 16 B.

4. 28 April 1980, MSA: I 95.

5. Letter to Rebecca Quinn, 30 April 1980, MSA: C 69.

6. Cesar Jerez SJ, letter to JMN, 8 July 1981, MSA: 16 A.

7. Ibid.

8. Letter to Catherine Verbeten OP, 16 July 1980, MSA: C 89.

9. Ita Ford MM, "Some Reflections Six Weeks After Arrival In El Salvador..." 1 June 1980, MSA: I 102.

10. Ibid.

11. Carla Piette MM, letter to Rebecca Quinn MM, 17 May 1980, MSA: C 76.

12. Ibid.

13. 12 May 1980, MSA: C 72.

14. 7 June 1980, MSA: I 104.

15. Letter to Katherine Gilfeather MM, 30 July 1980, MSA: C 93.

16. 29 May 1980, MSA: I 100.

17. 11 June 1980, MSA: I 105.

18. Letter to Jackie Hansen Maggiore, 15 June 1980. MSA: C 81.

19. Ita Ford MM, letter to Marie Giblin MM, 15 June 1980, MSA: I 107.

20. Rody, MSA: 16 B.

21. Letter to Catherine Verbeten OP, 16 July 1980, MSA: C 89.

22. "Three Months Experience in El Salvador," MSA: 17 C.

23. Ibid.

24. Patricia Haggerty MM, interview with JMN, 17 June 1981, MSA: 16 C.

25. Ibid.

26. Rita Owczarek MM, interview with JMN, 14 September 1981, MSA: 6 H.

27. "Deathtrap; Thirteen Aliens Die In Desert," *Time* 116, no. 3 (July 21, 1980?); and "Death March in the Desert," *Newsweek* (July 21, 1980).

28. 13 July 1980, MSA: I 110.

14. "Receive Me, Lord"

1. Maura Clarke MM, letter to "Family and Friends," 28 July 1980, MSA: M 186.

2. 28 July 1980, MSA: M 186 a.

3. Teresa Alexander MM, "A few of my memories. . .," 11 February 1982, MSA: 16 D.

4. Letter to Mary Manning, 11 August 1980, MSA: M 188.

5. Ibid.

6. 14 August 1980, MSA: M 190.

7. 21 August 1980, MSA: M 198.

8. 11 August 1980, MSA: C 95; and letter to Catherine Verbeten OP, 16 July 1980. MSA: C 89.

9. 30 July 1980, MSA: C 93.

10. 16 August 1980, MSA: I 112.

11. 13 July 1980, MSA: M 110.

12. Christine Rody VSC interview with Joan Petrik MM, summer 1981, MSA: 16 B.

13. 11 August 1980, MSA: C 95.

14. Ita Ford MM, letter to the Sisters in Chile, 7 September 1980, MSA: I 117.

15. Ita Ford MM, tape to Mrs. Mildred Ford, 6? September 1980, MSA: 14 B. (Unless otherwise designated, the following quotes in this chapter are from this source.)

15. Carla's Grave

1. Ita Ford MM, tape to Mrs. Mildred Ford, 6 September 1980, MSA: 14 B. (Material until the next footnote is from this source.)

2. Cesar Jerez SJ, letter to JMN, 8 July 1981, MSA: 16 A.

3. Ibid.

4. Margaret Hanlon MM, "Notes on a trip to El Salvador, August 25-September 2, 1980," for JMN, 14 April 1981, MSA: 14 D.

5. Julie Miller MM, letter to JMN, 14 February 1982, MSA: 13 A.

6. 7 September 1980, MSA: I 116.

7. Letter to Mrs. Mildred Ford, 9 August 1981, MSA: 16 F.

8. Ita's tape to her mother, MSA: 14 B; and Ita Ford MM, letter to Catherine Verbeten OP, 12 September 1980, MSA: I 120.

9. 7 September 1980, MSA: I 119.

10. 23 September 1980, MSA: M 210.

11. Carolyn Lehmann MM, letter to JMN, 12 February 1982, MSA: 23 A.

12. Ita Ford MM, letter to Mrs. Mildred Ford, 13 November 1980, MSA: I 137.

13. Ita Ford MM, letter to Rose Guercio MM, 7 September 1980, MSA: I 118.

14. 17 October 1980, MSA: I 123.

15. 25 November 1980, MSA: I 140.

16. 18 November 1980, MSA: I 139.

17. Letter to Margaret Dillon MM, 22 November 1980, MSA: M 227; and letter to Patricia Haggerty, 20 November 1980, MSA: M 226.

18. 17 October 1980, MSA: I 123.

19. Madeline Dorsey MM, interview with JMN, July 1981, MSA: 16 K.

20. Letter to Jean Rearden Baumann, 27 October 1980, MSA: I 125.

21. Ita Ford MM, "Report to PANISA Regional Assembly," 22 November 1980, MSA: 17 D.

22. Jerez, MSA: 16 A.

23. Madeline Dorsey MM and Teresa Alexander MM, tape to the Maryknoll Sisters Congregation, 6 December 1980, MSA: I C; and Madeline Dorsey MM, interview with JMN, 26 February 1983, MSA: 16 J.

24. Dorsey, MSA: 16 J.

25. Letter to Carolyn Lehmann MM, 14 November 1980, MSA: I 138.

16. Flying Home

1. Maria Rieckelman MM, interview with JMN, 30 May 1981, MSA: 19 A.

2. Ibid.

3. Ibid.

4. Ibid.

5. Ita Ford MM, "Report to the PANISA Regional Assembly," 22 November 1980, MSA: 17 D.

6. Rieckelman, MSA: 19 A.

7. Maria Rieckelman MM, "Report to the Maryknoll Sisters' Community," 5 December 1980, MSA: 19 C.

8. Madeline Dorsey MM, interview with JMN, July 1981, MSA: 16 K.

9. Oscar Romero, "The Poverties of the Beatitudes: Force of True Liberation of the Pueblo," homily for 17 February 1980, MSA: 15 C.

10. Maria Rieckelman MM, Answers to "Questions For Maria Rieckelman," for Maryknoll Sisters Office of Social Concerns, 30 October 1981. (Following quotes relative to this incident are from the same source.)

11. Dorsey, MSA: 16 K.

12. John Dinges, "New Evidence on Missionaries' Deaths in El Salvador Suggests Official Plot," *Pacific News Service,* July 1981.

13. Rita Owczarek MM, interview with JMN, 14 September 1981, MSA: 6 H.

14. Beatrice Zaragoza MM, tape to JMN, August 1982, MSA: 6 1.

15. Julie Miller MM, letter to JMN, 14 February 1982, MSA: 13 A.

16. Dinges' article.

Appendix 1

1. The Commission on the Truth interviewed eyewitnesses, diplomats, senior commanders of the National Guard and the armed forces, members of the Maryknoll Order, relatives of the victims, lawyers for the defendants and the churchwomen's relatives, and a member of the court assigned to the case. In addition, the court dossier was reviewed and governmental and non-governmental reports were analyzed. Colonel Zepeda Velasco was invited, unsuccessfully, to testify on several occasions.

2. Rogers-Bowdler report, p. 10.

3. Ibid., pp. 13-14.

4. See the statement by Major Oscar Armando Carranza, who said that Colonel Eugenio Vides Casanova had ordered an investigation into the deaths of the churchwomen.

5. Harold R. Tyler, Jr., *The Churchwomen Murders: A Report to the Secretary of State,* 2 December 1983 (known as the Tyler Report), p. 22.

6. Ibid., pp. 29-30.

7. Ibid., p. 24. See also the judicial statement of Lizandro Zepeda, vol., 2, f. 266, 23 June 1982, where he reports that he interviewed one person per day and that no conclusions were reached, although several people were interviewed.

8. Judge Tyler concluded that Major Zepeda had probably informed Colonel Vides Casanova. Tyler Report, p. 26.

9. Ibid., pp. 31-32.

10. Ff. 102, 147-57.

11. See President Duarte's speech, televised on 10 February 1982.

12. Statement by Dagoberto Martínez, f. 132, vol. 3, 30 July 1983.

13. See vol. 5 of the court dossier, f. 26, "Decision of the jury," 24 May 1983. See also ff. 26 and 65, 24 May and 20 June 1984.

14. *The New York Times*, 25 May 1984, pp. 1 and 6.

15. On 16 December 1980, United Nations Ambassador Jeanne Kirkpatrick said: "I don't think the government (of El Salvador) was responsible. The nuns were not just nuns; the nuns were political activists. We ought to be a little more clear-cut about this than we usually are. They were political activists on behalf of the Frente and somebody who is using violence to oppose the Frente killed them." *Tampa Tribune*, 25 December 1980, pp. 23A and 24A, col. 1.

Secretary of State Alexander Haig testified as follows before the Foreign Affairs Committee of the House of Representatives: "I would like to suggest to you that some of the investigations would lead one to believe that perhaps the vehicle that the nuns were riding in may have tried to run a roadblock or may have accidentally been perceived to have been doing so, and there may have been an exchange of fire." See *Foreign Assistance Legislation for Fiscal Year 1982: Hearings before the House Committee on Foreign Affairs*, 97th Congress, First Session 163, 1981.

16. The day after the deaths, President Jimmy Carter suspended aid to El Salvador. *The New York Times*, 14 January 1981.

In April 1981, the United States Congress was considering aid to El Salvador. On 26 April, Embassy officials met with the Minister of Defense García and with Vides Casanova and told them that the failure to investigate the case was jeopardizing United States aid. On 29 April, members of the National Guard were arrested and $25 million in military aid was approved the next day. See: Di Vicenzo, Janet, project ed., *El Salvador: The Making of U.S. Policy, 1984-1988*, vol. 1.

17. Tyler Report, p. 63.